Benjamin Szold, Marcus Jastrow

Songs and Prayers and Meditations

For Divine Services of Israelites

Benjamin Szold, Marcus Jastrow

Songs and Prayers and Meditations
For Divine Services of Israelites

ISBN/EAN: 9783337103835

Printed in Europe, USA, Canada, Australia, Japan

Cover: Foto ©Lupo / pixelio.de

More available books at **www.hansebooks.com**

SONGS

AND

PRAYERS AND MEDITATIONS

FOR

DIVINE SERVICES OF ISRAELITES.

COMPILED BY B. SZOLD,

RABBI OF THE CONGREGATION OHEB-SHALOM, BALTIMORE.

TRANSLATED FROM THE GERMAN

BY M. JASTROW,

RABBI OF THE CONGREGATION RODEF-SHALOM.

PHILADELPHIA:
PUBLISHED BY THE TRANSLATOR.
1873.

Entered according to Act of Congress, in the year 1873, by
M. JASTROW,
in the Office of the Librarian of Congress, at Washington.

CONTENTS.

I. **PSALMS.** Nos. 1—21. Pages 1—11.
1. The Way of the Righteous. 2. The Dignity of Man. 3. The Glory of the Lord 4. The Law of God. 5. The Lord our Shepherd. 6. We want naught. 7. The King of Glory. 8. Mindful of my End. 9. Solace in Distress. 10. Prayer for Pardon. 11. O Lord, be gracious. 12. Joy in the Sanctuary. 13. Thanksgiving and Praise. 14. Up to the Mountains. 15. No Blessing without God. 16. With God there is Forgiveness. 17. Praise of Concord. 18. Evening Prayer. 19. God, the Shield of Israel. 20. In deep Distress. 21. Praise Him.

II. **PRAISES AND THANKSGIVINGS.** Nos. 22—56. Pages 12—28.
22. God in the Heaven and in the Heart. 23. With Praises come before Him. 24. Hallelujah! Sing in Chorus. 25. Sing with Joy. 26. Praise His Greatness. 27. The Wonders of Creation. 28. From Far and Near. 29. Loud through Creation. 30. I will praise thee. 31. Thy grace, O Father. 32. God's Truth. 33. Praise, Israel. 34. Praise ye the Lord. 35. Great is the Lord. 36. The God of Love. 37. The Lord is God. 38. Great is the Lord. 39. Sing to the Lord. 40. Adonai, Praise and Honor. 41. Almighty God. 42. Praise and Glory. 43. Blessed be the Lord. 44. We praise Thee. 45. Holy art thou, God. 46. The Heavens proclaim. 47. The Heavens teach. 48. Nature's Realm. 49. Who form'st the Light. 50. Golden Beams. 51. All proclaim the Lord. 52. A Hallelujah. 53. Kedushah of Moses Ib'n Ezra. 54. Where shall I find thee? 55. The Lord of All. 56. The Doctrines of Faith.

III. **SOLACE AND HOPE.** Nos. 57—84. Pages 29—42.
57. What fear'st thou? 58. Ne'er despond. 59. Why sorrow'st thou? 60. Why criest thou? 61. Heavenward. 62. Seek ye the Lord. 63. Thou Holy One. 64. We worship thee. 65. Though dark my Night. 66. The Seed of Tears. 67. One Father, One Home. 68. Fear not. 69. Hope, the Golden Ladder. 70. Peace, my Heart. 71. My Heart. 72. If God be with me. 73. Not for a Long Life. 74. Hear our Prayer. 75. For thee, O Lord. 76. Father, I call on thee. 77. Lord, out of the depth. 78. God sleeps and slumbers not. 79. The Earth-imprisoned Soul. 80. In Holy Longing. 81. The God of Israel. 82. O Father, hear. 83. The Almighty's Kindness. 84. What God does, is in Bounty done.

IV. INSTRUCTION AND DEVOTION. Nos. 85—106.
Pages 43—54.
85. Deeds, but no Show. 86. God is my Stay. 87. Religion, God hath given. 88. Word of Life. 89. Truth and Peace. 90. The Torah a Light. 91. The Word of God refreshes. 92. The Light of God. 93. Mind and Will. 94. Lord, thy Laws. 95. God's Word is perfect. 96. Light and Truth. 97. Heart, Spirit and Power. 98. The Word of Revelation. 99. The Unity of God. 100. In deep Devotion. 101. What Religion teaches. 102. Arise, my Soul. 103. True Devotion. 104. The Breath of Holy Prayer. 105. I trust in thee. 106. Sh'ma Yisrael.

V. HYMNS FOR SABBATHS AND FESTIVALS. Nos. 107—139. Pages 55—77.
107. Sabbath Eve. 108. Sabbath Night. 109. The Day of Rest. 110. Sabbath Rest. 111. Sabbath, Peace-inviting. 112. Sabbath Morning. 113. Spring and Freedom. 114. The Days of Old. 115. Pessach Morning. 116. The Spirit of the Age. 117. Praise our God. 118. God, my Strength. 119. Mount of God. 120. This Day. 121. On Sinai's Top. 122. Up, to the Lord. 123. Lord our Creator. 124. Years like Rivers. 125. Days and Years. 126. Child's Repentance. 127. Lord, enthroned in Heaven. 128. Prayer for Peace. 129. The Memory of the Dead. 130. The Day declines. 131. The Peace of Neilah Evening. 132. Thy Works proclaim. 133. Life a Pilgrimage. 134. Festive Wreath, and Human Mission. 135. With Festive Wreaths. 136. Joys of Devotion. 137. This is the Torah. 138. Firmness in Faith. 139. My Salvation's Tower.

VI. THE SEASONS OF THE YEAR. Nos. 140—145.
Pages 78—80.
140. The Beneficence of the Lord. 141. Spring. 142. Summer. 143. Autumn. 144. Winter. 145. Nature, God's Witness.

VII. SONGS FOR THE CONFIRMATION ACT. Nos. 146—152. Pages 81—87.
146. Moment Most Holy. 147. Be blessed, O Lord. 148. Our Lips shall praise Thee. 149. The Teachings of the Lord. 150. We pray. 151. Grateful Praises. 152. Come, ye Children.

VIII. FOR THE THANKSGIVING DAY. Nos. 153—155.
Pages 88—90.
153. The Thanks of all Living. 154. The Mercies of the Lord. 155. Our Country.

PRAYERS AND MEDITATIONS.
On the Eve of the New Year, p. 91. Before sounding the Shofar, p. 94. For the Memorial Service for the Dead, p. 96. Prayers for various Occasions, p. 99. For the Confirmation Rites, p. 102.

SONGS FOR DIVINE SERVICES.

I.
PSALMS.

The Way of the Righteous.
(Psalm 1.)

Blest he who ne'er consents
  By ill advice to walk,
Nor stands on sinners' ways,
  Nor sits where scoffers talk.

But in the Law of God
  He finds his sole delight,
And in its thoughts employs
  His mind by day and night.

He shall be like a tree
  From watercourses fed,
That yields its fruit in time,
  Unfading leaves o'erhead.

2. The Dignity of Man.
(Psalm 8.)

O Lord, thy majesty is throned in heaven,
  And on the earth beneath thy name is glorious;
Yea, homage is to thee by tender sucklings given;
  Through lisping lips thy reign is made victorious.

When I behold the heavens thou hast fashioned,
   And all the marvels round, wrought by thy finger,
The moon, the stars, each on its watch-post stationed,
   Bowed down in awe before thee, Lord, I linger.

Oh! what is mortal man, that thou'rt commanding
   Unbounded gifts from heaven to surround him?
Yet, next to angels thou hast made his standing;
   With honor and with glory thou hast crowned him.

Hast made him Ruler;—all the world he swayeth.
   What lives on land, in air, to him thou'st given;
To him the sea, with all therein, obeyeth.—
   How glorious is thy name on earth, in heaven!

3. The Glory of the Lord.
(Psalm 19.)

The heavens are telling their Maker's glory,
   The firmament displays
   The wonders of his works.

One day to the other telleth the tale,
   And night unto night
   Gives knowledge of him.

O'er all the earth their word goes forth,
   Never unperceivèd,
   Ever understood.

The heavens are telling their Maker's glory,
   The firmament displays
   The wonders of his works.

4. The Law of God.
(Psalm 19.)

God's law is whole; come, soul, when ailing
   Find here the cure for thee designed;
His testimony is unfailing,
   Gives wisdom to the simple mind.

The Lord's commands are straight, unveering,
    His statutes—sunshine clear and bright;
The heart of man with comfort cheering,
    Enlightening the feeblest sight.

The fear of God is time-enduring,
    A living fountain pure and fair;
And his decrees are heart-assuring,
    A store of truth laid up for e'er.

They're higher prized than golden treasures,
    And more than honey are they sweet;
Be they my guides in woes, in pleasures,—
    Who keeps them shall with blessings meet.

---

5.   **The Lord our Shepherd.**
(Psalm 23.)

Our Shepherd is the Lord,
    And we the flock he feedeth;
His earth, with beauty stored,
    Yields all that mankind needeth.

Is there a thirsting heart,
    His staff to waters leads it;
To soothe its aching smart,
    With joy and light he feeds it.

Through night of death and dread
    We walk, and never tremble;
By our good Shepherd led,
    We know we shall not stumble.

His light is bliss and health,
    In it we find salvation;
His comfort is our wealth,
    Be high or low our station.

Songs for Divine Services.

6.   We want naught.
(Psalm 23.)

How shall from want I ever suffer,
    When God my Shepherd feedeth me,
He makes me lie where meadows offer,
    And by still waters leadeth me.

What heals my aching heart, he knoweth,
    He knows to comfort, knows to bless;
He for his holy name's sake showeth
    To me the path of righteousness.

What if I pass the vale where, lightless,
    Dire Death resides? I'm not afraid.
Thou art with me—that makes me frightless—
    Thy comfort is my staff, my aid.

7.   The King of Glory.
(Psalm 24.)

Lift up your heads,
And open full wide,
Ye gates of the world,
That the King of Glory may enter.
Who is the King of Glory?
The Lord strong and mighty!
Strong and mighty in battle.
Who is the King of Glory?
God Zebaoth,—
He is the King of Glory.

8.   Mindful of my End.
(Psalm 39.)

Lord, make me know my end, and let me, mortal,
    Think of this span of life, how short it is,
That when thy call invites me to thy portal.
    I may come forth with deeds of lasting bliss.

For all that is of earth must fade,
And man is but a fleeting shade,
If to the Dead he gives his heart,
Forgetful of his living part.

On thee alone let all my joys be founded;
  O Lord, unto my call incline thine ear,
That I with help and comfort be surrounded.
  For, lo! I am a stranger with thee here;
    A traveller o'er this life's main
    Of grief and trouble, toil and pain,
    Of sorrow, labor, woe and care;
    O, make me hope in thee fore'er!

---

9. **Solace in Distress.**

(Psalm 42.)

Tell me, my soul, what aileth thee?
  Why on thy hopes this blight?
O heart, my heart, what grieveth thee?
  Wherefore this tongueless fright?
    To God, thy Father, flee,
      On him, on him rely!
    He will deliver thee,
      Rely! rely!

My Father! hear my anxious cry;
  So direful is my dole!
Why did thy love forget me, why?
  O come to bless my soul!
    To God, thy Father, flee,
      On him alone rely!
    He will deliver thee,
      Rely! rely!

Songs for Divine Services.

10.   **Prayer for Pardon.**
(Psalm 51.)

Lord, hear me in thy tender grace,
   Accept thy servant's meek confessions;
I have my guilt before my face,
   I cannot gainsay my transgressions.—
Lord, cleanse me, cleanse me from my sin,
   That I in gladness be thy servant;
Give me a guileless heart within,
   Renew my spirit firm and fervent.

---

11.   **O Lord, be gracious.**
(Psalm 67.)

O Lord, be gracious unto us,
   And with thy blessing speed us,
Let shine thy face illustrious;
   To life eternal lead us.

That we may heed thy ways with awe,
   And follow e'er thy teaching,
Thus the salvation of thy Law
   To all the nations preaching.

All nations shall, O Lord, confess
   Thy never-ending glory,
Acknowledging thy righteousness,
   With joy appear before thee.

Yea, righteously thou governest
   And judgest every nation,
Let us fore'er securely rest,
   O Lord, in thy salvation!

12. Joy in the Sanctuary.
(Psalm 84.)

How goodly are thy habitations!
  My soul desired—it yearned to see,
O Lord of Hosts, these holy stations,
  The dwellings of thy majesty.
My body and my soul now laud
The ever living, bounteous God.

Lo, as the sparrow finds a building,
  And as the swallow rears a nest,
From storms her tender offspring shielding,
  So I fly to thine altars blest.
Blest he who in thy house may dwell,
Allowed alway thy praise to tell.

Thou art a shield, a sun, emitting
  Bright rays of glory and of grace,
With joy and happiness outfitting
  All those that walk before thy face.
O Lord of Hosts, throned in the skies,
How blest he who on thee relies!

---

13. Thanksgiving and Praise.
(Psalm 100.)

Attune God's praise, serve him with joy all earth,
Come all before his face with holy mirth!
  Acknowledge ye, that we by him are bred,
  His sheep we are, the flock he e'er has fed.

O, enter then his gates with grateful song,
And move with praises all his courts along;
  Give thanks to him to whom all praise is due,
  For he is ever gracious, ever true.

14. Up to the Mountains.
(Psalm 121.)

I lift mine eyes up to the mountains, sighing,
  "Is there no help unto me given?"
My help springs from a fountain never drying,
  From him who made the earth and heaven.
Behold, he slumbers ne'er, he sleepeth ne'er,
Who watches Israel with loving care.

---

15. No Blessing without God.
(Psalm 127.)

If God build not the house, in vain
  The builders spend their toil and pain;
If God shield not the town, in vain
  The watchmen from night's sleep abstain.
In vain ye rise with morning's light,
And sit up late, to eat by night
  The bread of care.—He granteth rest
  To those who with his grace are blest.

---

16. With God there is Forgiveness.
(Psalm 130.)

Out of the depths, in pain and care,
  I send my cry up unto thee;
Incline thine ear and hear my prayer,
  My earnest suit, Lord, answer me.
If thou shouldst mark the trace of sin,
Lord, who could hope thy grace to win?
  But, lo, from thee is pardon given,
  That man may dare look up to heaven.

I hope in thee, my God.—My heart
In yearning would for heaven start.
  My soul looks out for thee in sorrow,
  More than the watchman for the morrow.—

Hope, Israel! Wherever sailing,
  Make him the compass of thy hope;
With him is mercy never-failing,
  And redemption in full scope.
The Lord of peace—he will efface
The sins of Israel, in his grace.

---

17.   **Praise of Concord.**
              (Psalm 133.)

How blest the sight, the joy how sweet,
When brothers joined with brothers meet,
  A mutual loving band!
How sweet the liquid fragrance, shed
On Aaron's consecrated head,
  From his own brother's hand,

When both were blessing, both were blest!—
Sweet as the dews from Hermon's breast
  On Zion's hills descend;
Her hills has God with blessings crowned,
There promised grace that knows no bound,
  And life that ne'er shall end.

---

18.   **Evening Prayer.**
              (Psalm 134.)

Come, bless ye the Lord,
  His servants, ye all
  Who in his house
Stand, with prayers and vows,
  At evening's solemn call.
Uplift ye your hands toward his abode,
  And sing the praise of God.
The Lord who has made both heaven and earth,
Will bless thee from Zion with holy mirth.

19. God, the Shield of Israel.
(Psalm 129.)

Had not the Lord stood by my side,
  When men against me rose:
I never, never could abide
  The wrath of all my foes.
As furious billows did they roll,
And roar to sweep away my soul.

Blest be the Lord, for he conferred
  On me his gracious care;
I have escaped them, as a bird
  That flies the fowler's snare.
The snare is broke, we are set free,—
Forever, Lord, I'll hope in thee.

In deep Distress.
(Psalm 143.)

O Lord, in care I meet thee;
  Behold my deep distress!
And let my prayer entreat thee
  In thy great faithfulness.
O, bid not thy poor servant
  Before thy court appear;
No man, however fervent,
  Can in thy sight be clear.
Sin hath destroyed my heaven,
  The peace within my breast;
With pangs my heart is riven,
  My spirit is depressed.

My soul within me fainteth,
   And wrings with grievous smart,
The night of anguish painteth
   Dark shadows in my heart.
My Father, I now call thee;
   O come, deliver me!
From passions that enthrall me
   To thee alone I flee.
Teach thou me in thy kindness,
   To serve thee all my days;
Without thee I'm in blindness;
   Lord, light me with thy rays!

---

21.   **Praise Him.**

(Psalm 150.)

Praise him who reigneth o'er us,
Praise him in songs sonorous,
Joined with high heaven's chorus,
Praise him whose deeds are wondrous,
   Whose greatness unexcelled;
   Loud praise his might, the infinite!—
Praise him with psalteries, praise him with trumpets,
   Praise him with chimes wide ringing,
   With harps and with timbrels,
   With chords and with organs,
   Shouting to the skies.
Praise him who reigneth o'er us,
   Praise him in songs sonorous,
   Joined with high heaven's chorus,
   Praise him whose deeds are wondrous,
   Whose greatness unexcelled!   Hallelujah.

II.
PRAISES AND THANKSGIVINGS.

22.   God in the Heaven and in the Heart.

Thou Only One, enthroned in heavens above,
  My light, my trust, my staff, my stay,—
    Thou rul'st o'er life and death.
Thou Only One, in thy abundant love,
  Thou deign'st to dwell in hearts of clay,—
    Thine be my latest breath!

---

23.   With Praises come before Him.

With praises come before him,
  Extol the God of might;
The heavenly choirs adore him,
  To him shout Day and Night.
Him praises all creation,
  All beings spread his fame;
O, Jacob's Congregation,
  Sing him with loud acclaim.
The Lord is God! To him cling,
  For perfect is his way,
The Lord is God! To him sing,
  My soul, for e'er and aye!

---

24.   Hallelujah! Sing in Chorus.

Hallelujah! Sing in chorus,
To his honor hymns sonorous;
  In his courts with mirth appear.
Bring him offerings, all ye mortals,
Come with joy into his portals,
  Bring him thanks, from far and near!

Should we not with anthems sing him,
And our lips' oblations bring him,
  Who sustains the world he framed?
Children, bow to him, be humble!
Though he sees us fail and stumble,
  Yet, his children are we named.

Come, draw near him, mortal creature!
Ne'er despond! Though frail thy nature,
  God is gracious, great his love.
Think the thought, so awe-inspiring!—
Feel the joy, to bring untiring
  Thanks to God enthroned above!

---

25.   **Sing with Joy.**

Sing with joy the God of grace,
  Praise him in his dwelling-place!
Grace he has bestowed upon us,
  Leading us in every age,
To the goal his staff has shown us,
  Stilling storms' and billows' rage.
Sing the wonders he has done us!
  Sing with joy the God of grace,
  In his dwelling-place!

---

26.   **Praise his Greatness.**

Praise his greatness, praise his power,
Let your thanks to heaven tower,
  With triumphant songs adore him,
  Come with thankful hearts before him;
    His great Name adore
    For evermore.

Praise the Ruler of all powers,
Praise his goodness, for he showers
   On us mercies none can measure.
Let your hearts breathe hallowed pleasure!
   His great Name adore
   For evermore. Amen.

27.   **The Wonders of Creation.**

When on thy power I meditate,
   And see thy wisdom's traces,
When I reflect thy love how great,
   That all mankind embraces:
O Lord, I linger, and I gaze,
And find no words to sing thy praise.
Where'er I turn, my eyes detect
   New wonders of creation;
The skies with sheeny splendors decked,
   Give thee, O Lord, ovation.
O God of might and majesty,
Thy name is bright eternally!

28.   **From Far and Near.**

Hallelujah!
O sing the Lord in holy fear,
Extol the Lord from far and near,
   In every age and time!
From North to South, from East to West,
His name be praised, his name be blest,
   In every land and clime!
Hallelujah!
Who durst with God, our Lord, compare?
A Savior in distress and care,
   From age to age the same.
He lends the pious strength and trust,
While wicked arms are crushed to dust,
   The Eternal is his name.
Hallelujah! Amen.

Songs for Divine Services.

29.   **Loud through Creation.**

Loud through creation sounds
   The glory of our God,
And, like a wave, redounds
   His praise in his abode.
Come, let us strike the harp and sing praise in accord,
   To the Lord, to the Lord.

Vain is the scoff of ruthless nations
   Who Israel oppose,
We bring our God ovations,
   In spite of threats, in sight of foes.
Him who ne'er endeth,
Whom no mind comprehendeth,
Him sing, proclaim his grace,
Here in his dwelling-place!
   Accord
Psalteries to the Lord.

---

30.   **I will praise thee.**

Thou art my Father, I will praise thee,
   Thy love shall claim my sweetest song;
To happiness thou didst upraise me,
   Thine be my harp, thine be my tongue.
To praise thy power that endeth never,
To praise thy wisdom I'll endeavor.
   I dedicate my song to thee,
   Thine be my lyre, my psaltery!

When I awake at early dawn,
   My soul soars up to thee above;
When night descends on field and lawn,
   My heart exalts thee, thrilled with love.
O, what delight in lays sonorous
To blend my voice with Nature's chorus!
   I dedicate my song to thee,
   Thine be my lyre, my psaltery!

In thee all my affections gather,
  To live in thee, O Lord, I yearn;
On wings of song, my Source, my Father,
  I fain would unto thee return.
My yearning shall with powers gift me
Unto thy heavens to uplift me.
  I dedicate my lyre to thee,
  Thine be my harp, my psaltery!

---

31.   **Thy Grace, O Father.**

When I behold thy grace, O Father,
  Each morning with the light renewed;
My throbbing heart longs to approach thee
  With words of love and gratitude
Thou guard'st me with a father's cares;
Thy love with all my frailties bears.

How many wonders of thy kindness
  In my own life may I descry!
Thy light is shed on all my footsteps,
  Thy love looks on me from on high.
O joy! I am of birth divine,
My spirit is a part of thine!

---

32.   **God's Truth.**

Arise, my soul, and wing thee
  Up to thy God above;
Give praise, and tell how kingly
  He pours on thee his love!

Display with grateful pleasure
  His truth in pious rhyme;
Thy psaltery's glad measure
  Shall praise the Most Sublime.

To praise him, it behooves thee,
　Whatever be thy dole;
Thy life is his, he loves thee;
　Forget it not, my soul!

---

33.   **Praise, Israel.**

Praise, Israel, the Lord whose might
　Is manifest in story,
In saving thee he had delight,
　Shout, Israel, his glory.
　　In grateful lays
　　Exalt his ways;
On virtue's path he guides us,
And in his mercy hides us.

---

34.   **Praise ye the Lord.**

Praise ye the Lord in his abode most holy,
Sing him songs in the stronghold of his might.
　　As thou at all times didst shower
　　　On thy works thy gifts of grace,
　　So will ne'er thy love and power
　　　Cease to lead the human race.
　For thy kindness ever true
　With each morning shines anew.

---

35.   **Great is the Lord!**

　Great is the Lord!
　He knows our weakness,
　And is with us in all our ways.
　　Good is the Lord!
　My soul, in meekness,
　　Give to thy Father's love due praise.
Praised be the Lord!

36. The God of Love.

My bosom is thine altar,
  Pure love my sacrifice,
The thanks, my lips are telling,
  With joy to thee arise.
Accept, O Lord, my offering,
  My prayer to thee above.
Nigh art thou to thy fearers,
  Thou art a God of love!
    Hallelujah!
Bring, my heart, bring him ovation,
  Tell his love with each pulsation!
    Hallelujah!

How often hast thou brightened
  With joys my path of life,
So wilt thou ever grant me
  To conquer in each strife.
Into thy hand, Almighty,
  Resigning mine estate,
I pray in meekness, "Rule thou,
  Lord, as thou wilt my fate."
    Hallelujah!
Give the God of love due praises,
When he lowers, when he raises.
    Hallelujah!

37. The Lord is God.

The Lord is God, the universe proclaims him,
Whate'er thou seest, whate'er thou hearest, names him.
  O, bend to him in awe!
  The Lord is God,
  He is a gracious God.

The Lord is God, he unto us hath given
The light of mind, the Law revealed from heaven;
    We bow to him with thanks.
    The Lord is God,
    He is a gracious God.

---

38.   **Great is the Lord.**

  Great is the Lord, and none beside;
    To him sing, all who fear him!
  Who is like him? who may abide
    His light, and who come near him?
      The Lord is great,
      His name is great,
    Wide open is his mercy-gate.
  How blest all who revere him!

---

39.   **Sing to the Lord.**

  Sing to the Lord a joyful strain!
    He is our God, none else!
    In clouds of mystery he dwells,
  The worlds are his domain.
    Great is his name!
  He wills—'tis wrought,
    Lo, there in pride it stands,
    And when his word of might commands,
  Soon all is turned to naught.

  He is the Love; in him rejoice;
    His choice is thine own best;
    His deeds are altogether blest,
  And truthful is his voice.

He reigns on earth!
He hears thee cry,
  And makes thy bosom still;
    If straight thy way, if good thy will,
Press on! the Lord is nigh.

Sing to the Lord a joyful strain!
  He is our God, none else!
  In clouds of mystery he dwells,
The worlds are his domain.
  Great is his name forevermore.—Amen.

40. Adonai, Praise and Honor.

Adonai, praise and honor
Be offered to thy name,
Until this hall formed by thy hand
Turn unto dust at thy command,
Shall in halls we've founded
The "Holy" be sounded.   Hallelujah.

41. Almighty God.

Almighty God, we sing thy praise,
Beneficent, we laud thy ways.
    The earth is thy majestic altar,
    The heavens are thy glory's psalter.
All living hope in thee, O Lord,
All living sing, Hallelujah!

42. Praise and Glory.

Praise give and glory unto our God;
For he is all-gracious;
Great above earth and heaven
Is his loving-kindness.

Praise give and glory unto our God!
Serve ye the Lord with joy and gladness,
Come ye with psalms before his presence.
Praise give and glory unto our God!

---

43.   **Blessed be the Lord.**

Bless'd be the Lord! In gladness I will sing him,
And hymns of thanks in joyful chorus bring him;
    In unison with all that walk before him,
        I will adore him.

Majestic are the works he hath created,
They tell his might, with holy mirth elated;
    They are to me a source of holy pleasure,
        Beyond all measure.

A book of wisdom, Lord, is thy creation,
I'll read in it with awe and admiration;
    Enlighten me, and let my reason choose thee,
        My heart not lose thee.

---

44.   **We praise thee.**

We praise thee, Lord, who mad'st the world thy tent;
    To thee on wings of song my soul is soaring;
O thou, residing in the firmament,
    To thee we bow in awe, thy grace imploring.

Who is like thee, so excellent in might?
    Who is like thee in glory, truth and splendor?
The heavens are thy throne, thy garb is light,
    Sun, moon and stars to thee their homage render.

Yet with a father's love thou look'st on earth,
    To mete thy mercies out to all thy creatures;
From thee all gifts, all joys of life spring forth,
    And man hast thou endowed with heavenly features.

45. Holy art thou, God.

Holy art thou, God,
Savior from affliction's flood,
   Thine is the might;
   The heavens are thy tent of light.—
At thy command,
In pride and resplendence all things stand,
   To delight man's wondering sight;
   Lord, our God, thy name is holy!

---

46. The Heavens proclaim.

The heavens proclaim their Master's glory,
   Their voices bear his fame abroad;
Him praise the lands, him laud the oceans,
   Hear man, with awe, the voice of God!
Who guides the numberless hosts of heaven?
   Who wakes the Sun from nightly rest?
He goeth forth like a valiant hero,
   To run his race from East to West.

Come, man, and view the wonders of nature
   To thine astounded sight unfurled,
See power and wisdom swaying their scepter,—
   Proclaim they not the God of the world?
He is thy Maker, he is the mercy,
   And he is thy salvation's fount;
Love him, love him in thy heart's profoundness,
   Among his chosen ever count.

---

47. The Heavens teach.

The heavens teach, O Lord, thy praises,
   The earth is witness of thy might,
The voice which all creation raises,
   Resounds by day, is heard by night.

Where'er I turn my gaze astounded,
  I see a father's watching love;
Thus by thy witnesses surrounded,
  I send my praise to thee above.

---

48.   **Nature's Realm.**

Lord, thy greatness and thy power,
  Are in Nature's realm revealed,
Countless are thy gifts that shower
  Down on forest as on field.

Therefore, songs of praise wide-sounding,
  Rise from every lip beneath,
Echoes of thy grace, rebounding
  From the hearts of all that breathe.

---

49.   **Who form'st the Light.**

Who form'st the light, mak'st everything,
  Thou fount of all salvation,
On every morn, O holy King,
  Renewing thy creation—

As hosts of fervent angels praise
  Thine excellence, thy splendor,
We sing thee for these morning rays,-
  For all thy mercies tender.

---

50.   **Golden Beams.**

The sun each morning greets
  With golden beams the ocean,
And every wave he meets
  Reflects the glistening motion.

Thine eye, Lord, on me dwells,
  My heart waves like the ocean,
Reflects thy look and tells
  Thy grace in joy's emotion.

---

51.   **All proclaim the Lord.**

Lord, all proclaim thy name:—
  The sun above that glows,
The lightning's flashing flame,
  The golden blooming rose,
The fowl with tinges tender—
  What glitters, gleams and glows,
Reflects, O Lord, thy splendor.
  The sun in my heart glows,
  In me the warbler sings,
  In me the flower blows.
What up to heaven rings,
  What down from heaven blazes,—
My heart feels it and grows
  And swells in grateful praises.

---

52.   **A Hallelujah.**

The Lord, the Lord, the Ruler, Almighty,
  The King is he alone,
  Creation is his throne;
  He reigns, besides him none.
The Lord shall reign for ever and ever.
Lord of all, and King of kings,
Thou rulest ever and ever!
  Hallelujah.

Songs for Divine Services.

53.   **Kedushah of Moses Ib'n Ezra.**

By angels in heaven
The Lord is given
  Glory and fame.
Celestial hosts
Stand on their posts
  To praise his name.
Above, beneath,
Lo, all that breathe,
  With awe proclaim,
" Holy, holy, holy
Is the Lord of Hosts."

With fear impressed,
They never rest
  To sing his might;
The Seraphim
Give praise to him,
  With flashing light.
The earthly choirs
With sacred fires,
  Shout to his height,
" Holy, holy, holy
  Is the Lord of Hosts."

Around his throne,
His servants own
  His power in fear.
With thunder's voice
They all rejoice
  In the heavenly sphere.
The heavens round
Repeat the sound
  From far and near:
" Holy, holy, holy
Is the Lord of Hosts!"

54. Where shall I find thee?

(After the Hebrew of Jnda Halevi.)

O Lord, where shall I find thee,
  Whose seat no eye espies?
And where, O Lord, not find thee,
  Whose throne is earth and skies?

Who dwell'st in hearts that fear thee,
  To worlds thou sett'st a bar;
Thou shield of all who're near thee,
  And staff of those afar!

O thou 'mong Cherubs dwelling,
  Enthroned in ether's light,
All praises they are telling
  Can never reach thy height.

And yet, midst sons of earth, here,
  Should God dwell? Daring thought!
A dream how high aspiring
  Of man who is like naught!

Yet, where thy praise resoundeth,
  Thy majesty is near,
From heaven to earth reboundeth
  The song of holy fear.

55. The Lord of all.

The Lord of all was sovereign King,
  Ere aught that is was moulded;
Now that all nature stands in pride,
  The worlds display his kingdom.

And he is one, besides him none,
  With none he shares his glory;
Has no beginning and no end,
  His are the power and kingdom.

He is my God, my Savior he,
  My Rock, my Stay in anguish;
He is my refuge and my flag,
  My cup, my share forever.

Unto his hand I trust my soul,
  When sleeping, when awaking,
And with my soul my body's frame;
  He is with me, I fear no evil.

---

56.   **The Doctrines of Faith.**

Attune the song of holy truth!
God *is;* bow down, old age and youth!

And he is One!—Raise up your hands!
His unity—who understands?

Spiritual and figureless,
Unequalled he in holiness!

All things through him exist alone,
But he himself hath ne'er begun.

On earth, in heaven, everything
Tells, he is the Almighty King.

Prophetic truth he did inspire
Into the men of sacred fire.

He made his grace on Moses shine;
No prophet was like him divine.

Through him, the Shepherd, true and tried,
He gave the Law as Judah's guide.

Let systems change and doctrines fall,
The Law of God surviveth all.

To him is known the thought of the heart,
The end of things, ere yet they start.

What through thy deeds thou here may'st earn,
Thy judge will on thy head return.

Redemption comes, all troubles end
Of those who on his help depend.

The night of death he turns to day;
Blest be his name fore'er and aye!

III.

SOLACE AND HOPE.

57.   **What fear'st thou?**

What fear'st thou? God rules earth and skies,
    He knows all thy affairs.
What even men as small despise,
    Escapeth not his cares.
        His eyes—they sound
        Thy heart's profound;
He knows thy wishes, knows what grieves thee,
He stills thy anguish and relieves thee.

---

58.   **Ne'er despond!**

Ne'er despond! Though clouds may hover,
    Threat'ning to obscure thy day;
Hands unseen protecting cover
    Thee, O feeble son of clay!

Ne'er despond! Though sorrows cumber
    With their weighty load thy heart;
Yet, thou know'st there comes a slumber;
    And all troubles will depart.

Ne'er despond! Though soon life's flower
    Fade, and dimness cloud thy eye,
Death hath over thee no power,
    What is Godlike cannot die.

59. Why sorrow'st thou?

Tell, my soul, why sorrow'st thou?
Why this trembling fear within?
  Lives there not a God above us,
Watching o'er us day and night?
  Know'st thou not that he doth love us,
Love us ever, though he smite?
      Look on high,
      God is nigh;
      Heavenward raise,
      Man, thy gaze!
Every tear that dews thy cheek,
Counteth he who loves the meek.

Tell, my soul, why sorrow'st thou?
Why this trembling fear within?
  Is, then, thy bereavement endless?
Art thou in this world alone?
  Lov'st thou nothing? Art thou friendless?
Is there naught to call thine own?
      God is thine,
      Do not pine!
      All thy days
      Walk his ways,
For his faith shall ne'er decay,
Ne'er his fount of love betray.

---

60. Why criest thou?

Why criest thou, my heart, in sorrow?
  Why criest thou and sigh'st "Alas!
O Lord my God, when comes the morrow?
  When will that night, that long night pass?
That marsh-light glittering from afar,
When will it prove a truthful star?"

O Lord my God! Truth is thy essence;
    Thou art the mercy, thou the tree
Of life; clear light is in thy presence,
    Wise counsel, Father, is with thee.
Bid twilight vanish, dusk and drear,—
    Let morning's rosy mirth appear!

O Lord, thou fount of life e'er flowing,
    Thou never-fathomed sea of love,
Give me, to quench my thirst so glowing,
    One wave, one drop from thee above.
O, still the thirst that burns in me,
    O, hush my soul that yearns for thee!

---

61.   **Heavenward.**

Heavenward our paces lead;
    On this earth we are sojourning,
And to Canaan, as our meed,
    Through the desert we are turning.
Here on dusty roads we roam,
Yonder, yonder is our home.

Heavenward! My faith in God
    Pointeth to the land eternal.
Soaring is my soul abroad,
    Far beyond the lights supernal.
I am longing to return
Where the lights of beauty burn.

Heavenward when taking me,
    Loving Death shall find me quiet;
Then I'll look triumphantly
    Down on all this earthly riot.
Heavenward my soul shall strive,
Till at last I there arrive.

Songs for Divine Services.

62   **Seek ye the Lord.**

Seek ye the Lord, and he is near,
Call ye on him, and he will hear.
  Look up to him—
    In darkness a light—
  Hope ye in him,
    By day and by night.

Seek ye the Lord, and he is near,
Call ye on him, and he will hear.
  He is the love,
    Though e'en he try us,
  He, from above,
    Cheereth the pious.
Seek ye the Lord, and he is near,
Call ye on him, and he will hear.

---

63.   **Thou Holy One.**

Look down on us who stand here bowed and humble,
  Thou Holy One, who guard'st the infant's life;
Assist us in our need! let us not stumble;
  Make us victorious in our strife.
    From sorrow's rod
      Guard us, O God!
    To thee we pray,
      Our Rock, our Stay;
    With fervent hearts we **pray,**
  Be our guard for aye!
  O, hear our suppliant lay!

---

64   **We worship thee.**

We worship thee, O Lord, with awe,
  Who rulest earth and heaven.
Our life is brief—this is thy law—
  To thee be praises given!

The wreath of youth will fast decay,
The fire of youth will die away,
  Thou rul'st, thou reign'st forever.

We lean, O Lord, upon thy grace,
  Our days are few and grievous;
Like clouds that pass and leave no trace,
  The joys of life may leave us:—
Thou wert our father's shield and guard,
And wilt to us thy love award;
  Thou lov'st and blessest ever.

From dust to heaven points our faith,
  When soul and body sever;
To heaven leads the spirit's path,
  Her treasures vanish never.
O Hope, thou child of heavenly birth!
There is a life beyond this earth!
  Thy kingdom lasts forever.

---

65.   **Though dark my Night.**

Though dark my night, and o'er me break
  With flashing light the thunder;
I'm not afraid—God is awake
  To tear the clouds asunder.

His eyes behold my aching smart;
  In kindness does he number
The sorrows cumbering my heart,—
  The cares that break my slumber.

I know, he sent me trials, lest
My heart grow slothful when at rest,
  From God and virtue turning.
Awake, my soul, have God in sight;
Soon disappears the gloomy night,
  And rosy glows the morning.

66. The Seed of Tears.

What with weeping thou hast sown,
  Blooms and ripes, of joy the root;
If with labor thou hast mown,
  Cheerful shalt thou eat the fruit.

All the pious and the noble,
  Seeing lights that never cease,
Had to pass through strife and trouble,
  Climbing up the heights of peace.

Bear, O soul, thy pains with patience,
  Quiet walk the line of life,
When enough here thy probations,
  Blessings will reward thy strife.

---

67. One Father, one Home.

One loving Father have we all;
  'Tis God, whole holy pleasure
Created all, the great and small;
  His mercy has no measure.

One home paternal have we all,
  To which our ways are wending;
It is above—in yonder hall
  Of happiness unending.

---

68. Fear not.

Fear not, when thy sun is setting,
  When thy lot seems dark and dread;
Murmur not, and be not fretting,
  Though thou eat affliction's bread.

Songs for Divine Services.   35

> For the hand that gave thee sadness,
>   Holds of life and death the cup,
> Gives alike both woe and gladness,
>   Bringeth low and raiseth up.

---

69.   **Hope, the Golden Ladder.**

Hope! Hope is the golden ladder
  Whereon hearts to heaven climb;
Soul, take her for thy companion,
  Till thine hour of death shall chime.

When the morn serene and smiling
  Shines on life's awaking prime;—
When gray Sorrow calls on manhood,
  Covering its head with rime,—
When at last the age-worn traveller
  Asks, "When comes my resting time?"—

Hope is e'er the golden ladder
  Whereon hearts to heaven climb;
Soul, take her for thy companion,
  Till thine hour of death shall chime.

---

70.   **Peace, my Heart.**

Peace, my heart! Be still within,
  Though the night around be fearful;
Unless grieved by thine own sin,
  Lift thy head up free and cheerful!
Bright and righteous is God's path;
Hope, my heart, nor lose thy faith.

Heart, be trustful; not in vain
  Smites thy Father, nor to pain thee;
E'en thy suffering is thy gain,
  And through trials he will train thee.
Faith in God and future life
Conquers in all woe and strife.

Hope, my heart, and trustful keep;
  Soon to haven comes thy vessel,
When the raging billows sleep,
  And the tempests cease to wrestle.
Hark! God calls within thy breast,
"*There*'s the port that gives thee rest."

71. My Heart.

My heart, what is it then that blasteth
  Thy hopes, when God afflicteth thee.
Be blithe, my heart; not long it lasteth;
  Thy trouble ends, thou art set free.

Accept, my heart, God's dispensation,
  Whate'er he send thee from above;
For thy own best is thy probation,
  In trials he bestows his love.—

Yea, Father, I will still, unfearing,
  Go onward carrying my load,
My praying hands to thee uprearing,
  My hopeful eyes to thee, my God.

72. If God be with me.

If God be with me, I'll not shake
  In need and gloomy care;
The anchor of my hope may break,—
  I find my trust in prayer.
To thee alone, my God, I bend,
  Though men against me gather;
To happiness my ways shall tend,
  Thou art with me, my Father!

73.   Not for a Long Life.

I pray thee not my days to lengthen;—
A staff of trust my walk to strengthen,
  A levelled path, devoid of sorrow,
  Contentment new on every morrow,
Joined with a lofty aspiration
For spreading blessings and salvation,
  A gentle heart, devotion fervent—
  These gifts, O Lord, grant to thy servant.

---

74.   Hear our Prayer.

Hear our prayer, thou our Protector!
  Be propitious as we call;
Be our guardian and director
  Of our steps; let us not fall!
Not for empty show we care;
Grant that virtue be our share.

Lord, direct our inclinations,
  That to thee we may be true;
Far from glittering ostentations,
  Still and glad our ways pursue.
So thou dwellest in our heart,
Joys and pleasures are our part.

---

75.   For thee, O Lord.

For thee, O Lord, all beings wait,
  To give to them their daily alms.
  Thou openest thy hand,
  Their wants are satisfied.

Thou for a moment hid'st thy face,
    They tremble all and stand appalled;
    Thou tak'st their breath away,—
    Back to their dust they turn.

Again, thou send'st thy spirit forth,
    They are renewed and blossom fresh;
    Replenished is the earth
    Again with beauty's charms.

76.   Father, I call on thee.

Father, I call on thee!
Dangers unnumbered hourly expect me;
Lord, in thy mercy, thou wilt protect me.
    God of Creation, I call on thee,
    Father, O guide thou me!

Father, O guide thou me!
Guide me through life, and in death guide me;
Lord, to thy mercy I will confide me;
    Lord, as thou wilt, so guide thou me,
    Father, thy hand I see—

Father, thy hand I see!
Or in the leaflets' autumnal rustling,
Or in the storm-wind furious bustling,
    Fountain of mercy, thy hand I see;
    Father, O bless thou me!

Father, O bless thou me!
Thine is my life, Lord, thou didst awake it,
Thou who hast given, thou may'st take it,
    In life or in death, Lord, bless thou me;
    Father, I worship thee!

77. Lord, out of the Depth.

Lord, out of the depth, I call on thee!
  Father, hear me,
    Come to cheer me;
Lift thy countenance up to me!

Lord, to thee my eyes look up and wait.
  I implore thee,
    Come, restore me,
Ope to me thy mercy's gate!

---

78. God sleeps and slumbers not.

God sleeps and slumbers not,
  E'er open are his eyes.
He granteth thee thy lot
  In equal site and size.

God sleeps and slumbers not,
  His mercy's sun is bright;
When night besets thy cot,
  He will illume thy sight.

God sleeps and slumbers not,
  What day his angel lowers,
And from this darksome spot
  Thy soul to light upsoars.

---

79. The Earth-imprisoned Soul.

When the Lord unbars thy prison,
  All these earthly woes are fled,
As when thou from sleep arisen
  Thinkest of a nightmare's dread.
Yon, above the heavens starred,
Is thy joy in God unmarred.

What we here have sown in sadness,
  We shall reap in joy above;
There matures the fruit of gladness,
  In the balmy breeze of love.
Joyous garners he the grain,
Who hath sown in grief and pain.

---

80.   **In Holy Longing.**

My soul in holy longing,
  Would mount, O Lord, to thee,
Thy people's great protector
  In all their misery.

Oft felt we as lone strangers,
  Bearing disgrace and shame;
Yet, we survived all dangers,
  Made strong by thy great name.

---

81.   **The God of Israel.**

O God of Israel, hear us!
On the wings of prayer our hearts soar up to heaven,
We acknowledge thy power supreme,
And thy mercy renewed each morn.
Thine, thine are our hearts!

O God of Israel, hear us!
Give ear to our petition!
Almighty, Beneficent, hear us!
Thine is the breath we're breathing,
Thine our heart's pulsations.

O God of Israel, hear us!
God, Omnipotent, full of mercy!
God, Redeemer, hear our petition,
Answer our prayer—
O, Israel's God! Amen.

82. O Father, hear.

O Father, hear my word,
  Wherewith I come before thee;
Look graciously, O Lord,
  On me, as I implore thee;
Incline thine ear with love
  Unto my prayer ascending;
Up to thy heavens above
  My feelings all are tending.

Thou look'st into my heart,
  Thine eye knows no restriction;
And when in grief I smart,
  Thou know'st all my affliction.
I trust in thee alone,
  I shall not be forsaken;
In woes I will not groan,
  My faith shall ne'er be shaken.

---

83. The Almighty's Kindness.

How great is the Almighty's kindness!—
  Is he a man who shuts his eyes,
And obdurate, in willful blindness,
  Forbids his song to God to rise?

No, till my soul and body sever,
  To scan his love be my life's aim;
The Lord has ne'er forgot me—never
  Shall I forget my Father's claim.

Lord, as thy love is never-ending,
  Let me remember this always,
Thus strengthening my efforts, tending
  To consecrate to thee my days.

Thy love shall heal my heart when smarting,
  And be in happiness my guide;
Assist me, when this life departing,
  In fearlessness mine hour to bide.

---

84. What God does, is in Bounty done.

What God does, is in bounty done;
  Just are his dispensations;
Though o'er sharp thorns I have to run,
  I wait for him in patience.
He is my God,
And, at his nod,
    My path becomes a garden;
    Let him, then, be my warden.

What God does, is in bounty done;
  But he knows what availeth.
The godless man may lonesome run,
  On God to lean he faileth.
New every morn
His grace is born,
    I put on him my sorrow,
    Confide to him my morrow.

What God does, is in bounty done;
  When sinking, this shall stay me.
Though on the stormy path I run,
  All views and hopes betray me,
My God is he,
He leadeth me
    At last into his garden;
    Let him, then, be my warden.

IV.

INSTRUCTION AND DEVOTION.

85.   **Deeds, but no Show.**

O Rock of Ages, gracious Lord,
Grant that the seed grain of thy word,
    Laid in our hearts, may strike deep root,
    And there mature a healthful fruit.

True faith, that health-recruiting power,
True faith, that life-renewing flower,—
    O, let it in our bosoms grow,
    Maturing deeds—no empty show.

---

86.   **God is my Stay.**

    God is my stay!
    His word for aye
        Shall be my staff unbending.
    In all my ways
    I see the rays,
        Lord, of thy love unending.

    Thy word is true!
    O, clear my view,
        That I perceive its soundness.
    And let me find
    Delight of mind
        In sounding its profoundness.

87. Religion, God hath given.

Religion, thou sweet child of heaven,
  Be to my heart e'er dear and blest;
Oft with despair it would be riven,
  When by the load of life oppressed;
But thou giv'st gladness to my soul,
  And lead'st me gently to my goal.

Thou giv'st me faith and strength in danger,
  And when I sink thou hold'st me up;
Unto the wearied travelling stranger
  Thou lend'st the trusty staff of hope,
Whereon he still and firmly leans
  When resting from life's toiling scenes.

Unto my soul in darkness groping,
  Thou show'st the lights that ever burn;
The heavens at thy word are oping,
  I see the everlasting morn.
O, living truth of heavenly birth,
  Thou lift'st from dust the son of earth!

88. Word of Life.

Of all founts thou art the clearest,
  Word of life! Of heavenly birth,
From afar with light thou cheerest
  All that seek thee in life's dearth.
When they like a willow wither,
  Scorched by sunbeams overhead,
Say'st thou, "Travellers, come hither,
  Rest here at my shady bed!"——
O, pour in my heart sweet pleasures,
  Bidding earthly pains be dead;
Nor withhold thy limpid treasures
  Till death's shroud is o'er me spread.

Songs for Divine Services.

89.   **Truth and Peace.**

God is my light!
  Truth, truth seeks my soul,
    She asks, " O, where is light?—"
  Seek whom all extol,
    With him the day is bright.
God is my light!

God is my joy!
  Peace, peace seeks my heart,
    Would fain with joy be blest—
  High Heaven is thy part,
    There find'st thou joy and rest.
God is my joy!

---

90.   **The Torah a Light.**

Where should I find
The light of mind
  Save in thy law from heaven?
Without thy word,
My heart, O Lord,
  Would with suspense be riven.

Thy word explains
All joys and pains
  The soul on earth here trieth;
It calls this life
The scene of strife,
  To gain what never dieth.

Enthroned in awe!
Allow thy law
  To be my holiest pleasure!
Make it my strength,
And my days' length,
  My share, my wealth, my treasure!

91. The Word of God refreshes.

Blest is whom thy word refreshes,
    Lord, who makes thy law his stay;
Blest is whom thy light, the precious,
    Guides when dark around his way.
Bless'd by all, to all a blessing,
    Cheerfully he runs his course;
        And when wearied,
        He is carried
To a fresh and quickening source.

Lord, the precepts thou hast given,
    To perceive them make us wise.
To our hearts give peace from heaven,
    Power to see unto our eyes.
Look with blessings down upon us,
    Lead us where health's fountain starts,
        In thy tender
        Mercy, render
Pure again and bright our hearts.

---

92. The Light of God.

Lord, high is the position,
    Thou hast to us assigned.
To guide us on our mission,
    Thou gav'st a light of mind,

That quells our rising anguish,
    And bids all fears remove;
Imparts to hearts that languish
    The fire of heavenly love.

In life, it goes before us
    Illumining our path;
In death, it shineth o'er us,
    A star of hope and faith.

Songs for Divine Services.

93. **Mind and Will.**

Lord, who didst on Sinai's hill
   Teach us how to walk before thee,
Strengthen us, and make our will
   Join our minds, that both adore thee.

Lord enthroned in Majesty!
   Let thy power work within us;
Let each heart belong to thee;—
   For thy holy service win us!

---

94. **Lord, thy Laws.**

Lord, thy laws whose worth unmeasured,
   Thy decrees pure and divine,—
In my heart they shall be treasured,
   There shall be their earth-built shrine.
For they dart, on every station
   Of my life, light in my heart,—
Lead me onward to salvation,—
   Bid me choose my better part.

---

95. **God's Word is perfect.**

Thy word, my God, is perfect, teaching
   Man's way and end, man's work and strife;
It shows to all that list its preaching
   The road of truth, the rod of life.

On all our ways it shines before us,
   And bids the clouds of doubt depart;
It holds the shield of mercy o'er us,
   And fills with trustfulness each heart.

O, still my longing from thy fountain
   Of truth, which brightens all, O Lord,
Who on devotion's holy mountain,
   Contemplate earnestly thy word.
O, bid thy hallowed source impart
   New strength and peace unto my heart.

96.   Light and Truth.

O Lord, hear in abundant mercy,
   Thy Congregation's sacred lays;
Grant us to trace thy holy footprints,
   And walk forever in thy ways.

Love and compassion are thy footprints,
   To follow them be our life's aim;
O, with a father's arm embrace us,
   And guard our souls from sin and shame.

O, source of life and truth unending!
   Cheer with thy light each pious heart;
Vouchsafe that on our earthly journey
   That light may ne'er from us depart.

97.   Heart, Spirit and Power.

Create, my God, a *heart* in me,
   That glows in pious love to thee;
   Pure and true—a sacred shrine,
   A dwelling-place of praise divine.

A *spirit*, Lord, to me impart,
To break all idols of my heart;
  Great, sublime—a fount of light,—
  Truth-perceiving, clear and bright.

A *power*, O Lord, in me create,
Achieving what is good and great;
  Strong and firm, to act untired,
  E'er with holy zeal inspired.

98.   The Word of Revelation.

In this ark of holy station
Rests the word of revelation;
  Let it, Lord, now be implanted
  In our bosoms, and there granted,
As a seed of good deed,
Fruits of godliness to speed.

To thy word of truth immortal,
Open thou our inmost portal;
  Grant us with delight to hear it,
  Grant that it illume our spirit;
Mild and clear, true and sheer,
Did thy word to us appear.

As the bud unfolds its centre,
When mild sunbeams seek to enter,
  So our soul to thy light turneth,
  To admit thy truth she yearneth.
In this gate radiate,
Word of God! For thee we wait.

99. The Unity of God.

Hear, Israel, this word:
"*One is God;* to none beside him
  Shalt thou bow in servant's awe."
That it might forever guide him,
  He to Judah gave this law.—
It is in darkest nights our light,
  In all distress our strength, our might.

The Eternal is our God!
He is Master of all Nature,
  And unbounded is his might.
Bring him praises, every creature,
  Sing his greatness day and night!
To him we look, to him, the One,
  In darkness, or when bright our sun.

The Lord is One, is One!
One, when he, kind like a father,
  Keeps the world in his embrace,
One, when he in anger rather
  Seems to hide from us his face.
His mercy reigneth at all times,
  He leads through death to blissful climes.

---

100. In deep Devotion.

We all in deep devotion now,
Unto thy throne, Most Holy, bow,
  To hear thy word expounded.
Make pure our hearts, and strong our will,
That, all our days, we may fulfill
  Thy laws, on wisdom founded.

Songs for Divine Services.

101. What Religion teaches.

Calm to be, when storms around us riot,
    When on fortune's raging billows tossed;
Blithe to be when thrust into disquiet,
    When the waves swell high, yet must be crossed;
      This teaches us, the sons of earth,
      Religion of celestial birth.

Glad in God to welcome every morrow,
    Every night to close our eyes serene;
Unto God resigning each our sorrow
    Still to wait, till better days be seen;
      This teaches us, the sons of earth,
      Religion of celestial birth.

While alive, to live content; when dying,
    Calmly for a fairer land to wait,
Where unfading love reigns, re-allying
    All whom here fell death did separate:
      This teaches us, the sons of earth,
      Religion of celestial birth.

---

102. Arise, my Soul.

Arise my soul, and wing thee
    Up to thy Father's throne;
My lips shall sing his praises,
    And make his mercies known.
Through Moses he hath given
    To us his law—a guide
That leadeth through life's journey
    All who in it abide.

I praise thee, Lord, I praise thee:
  Thou hast to us unfurled
A light that made thy people
  A blessing to the world.
My helper in all dangers,
  My trust in care and death!
A priest I will be ever
  Of Israel's holy faith.

103.   True Devotion.

Bowed in meekness I stand here,
  Filled with reverent emotion;
Father, open thou my ear,
  Grant me true and still devotion,
That thy word with wisdom feed me,
And the way to heaven lead me.

Vouchsafe that thy holy word,
  As it to my heart descendeth,
There mature, my Rock and Lord,
  Fruits of life that never endeth,
All my powers within me nerving,
That thy will I do, unswerving.

Let it be my guiding light,
  When the way is dark before me;
And my stronghold, when the night
  Of drear doubts impendeth o'er me;
My delight, my consolation,
When I leave this earthly station.

Songs for Divine Services.

104.   **The Breath of Holy Prayer.**

O Lord, the breath of holy prayer,
Uplifting me from earthly care,
  Moves through this sacred dwelling;
My soul fain would to heaven flee,
She wings herself up unto thee,
  The fount whence truth is welling.
    Fear and gladness,
    Hope and sadness,—
    Each emotion
    Flows and waves through my devotion.

The world may offer me a cup
Containing many a bitter drop—
  One gaze of thine,—the furrows
Of care are smoothed to ease,
Our hearts are soothed with heaven's breeze;
  Away are all our sorrows.
    Thou mak'st blessèd
    The depressèd;
    Thy direction
    Leadeth mortals to perfection.

---

105.   **I trust in thee.**

I trust in thee! A rock unmoved
  Midst ocean's waves is, Lord, thy word;
On it I lean. Thy laws are proved,
  The light of truth do they afford.—
A father art thou unto me;
Thy child knows it and trusts in thee.

106.   **Sh'ma Yisrael.**

    Give ear, O Israel!
O, hear the holy word of creed
    Thou didst receive, so clear, so bright,
On Sinai there ;—it was thy lead,
    It was thy light by day and night;
It went with thee thy life to heed.

    Give ear, O Israel!
The Lord is God, and none besides;
    In him alone thou seëst bright
The thought that in creation hides.
    From him receive thy law, contrite;
With him alone the truth abides.

    Give ear, O Israel!
In all thy ways acknowledge him;
    If light thy path, and clear and bright,
Or wrapt in sorrow drear and grim:
    He is thy hope; have him in sight,
Though e'en thy light of life grow dim.

V.

HYMNS FOR SABBATHS AND FESTIVALS.

(*Sabbath.*)

107.   **Sabbath Eve.**

Thou, Sabbath Eve, returnest
    To earth from heaven's height;
For thee in holy earnest
    My heart throbs with delight.

When down thy shadow glideth,
    How grows my soul so still!
The storm of sin subsideth,
    Waked is the pious will.

Methinks the heavens greet me
    And bring from toil release;
Come, Sabbath, thou shalt meet me
    With God and man in peace.

---

108.   **Sabbath Night.**

Angels on their pinious bring thee
    Down to us, O Sabbath Night;
Hymns of holy triumph sing thee,
    And each heart is filled with light.
Earthly cares no more possess us;
Thou, O Sabbath, com'st to bless us.

Sabbath Night! A thousand burning
    Starlets glisten in our hearts;
With thy sheen thou still'st our yearning,
    Mild and quickening are thy darts.
With thy radiant garment dress us;
Sabbath, from thy heavens bless us!

109.   **The Day of Rest.**

This is the Day of Rest!
    A holy yearning thrills my heart;
    For God's abode it bids me start,
Through blessings to be blest.

Adoring stand I here.
    O sacred joy, O secret thrill!
    As when a host of angels, still
And soft, to me draw near.

Through blessings to be blest,
    The pious to God's dwelling flock,
    And praise aloud their heavenly Rock,
"This is thy Day of Rest!"

110.   **Sabbath Rest.**

Sabbath Rest, be welcome.
    Come, God's covenant from above,
    Come, anew make known his love,
    Who sent thee to Judah's race—
    Sweetest token of his grace!

Sabbath Joy, be welcome!
    O, release the prayerful soul
    Sighing under cares' control;
    Breathe sweet joy into each breast;
    Bring us pure celestial rest!

Sabbath Peace, be welcome!
  Bid all worldly thoughts retire;
  Make our heart a sacred lyre,
  Tune our soul to sing God's law,
  Fill our mind with holy awe!

111.   **Sabbath, Peace-inviting.**

When the Sabbath, peace-inviting,
  Fills our hearts with sacred mirth,
When from heaven, soul-delighting
  Manna raineth down on earth:
Then, to song all sorrow yieldeth,
  Loud to God rings up the strain,
Heaven-born devotion wieldeth
  O'er each soul her reign again.—
Here where worshipers assemble,
  Where God's spirit 'mong us dwells,
Where all lips rejoicing tremble,
  And with thanks each bosom swells:
Here the dust-born man perceiveth
  That he is the child of God,
Chosen, when this earth he leaveth,
  There to live in truth's abode.

112.   **Sabbath Morning.**

Sun and Sabbath—both how pleasant,
  Are allied this morning!
Messengers of God are present,
  Lights of joy are burning!—

Melodies of thanks awake me;
Up to thee I will betake me,
  With filial love adore thee.
Lord, I'll praise thy name each morrow,
Bless thee, both in joy and sorrow,
  And ever walk before thee.   Amen.

Songs for Divine Services.

113. Spring and Freedom.

When the Sun of Spring awaketh,
   And his rays redeeming melt the snow;
When her fetters Nature breaketh,
   And her starry blooms in beauty glow:
Sweet and pleasant rings the chime,
Welcome, welcome, Vernal Time!

When the Sun of Freedom dashes
   With his fiery rod the tyrant's crown,
That his scepter no more lashes
   Nations hanging on his haughty frown:
Thundering, roaring, rings the chime,
Welcome, welcome, Freedom's Time!

Fairest of all vernal days,
   When the Lord, redeeming Israel's tribe,
Bade them "Bask in freedom's rays,
   And my wonders on your hearts inscribe."
All abroad now may it chime,
Welcome, welcome, Vernal Time!
Welcome, welcome, Freedom's Time!

---

114. The Days of Old.

The days of old arise before us,
   When out of Egypt's bondage-house
Thy people, a rejoicing chorus,
   Went forth with grateful songs and vows.
No fetters more enslaved them;
Thy mighty arm, Lord, saved them,
   That made bright light from darkness rouse.

With Freedom's Manna didst thou feed them,
  And bid them bask in Freedom's ray;
Thy sceptre mild should henceforth lead them,
  And tyranny no longer sway.
To walk in light before thee,
Till all mankind adore thee,—
  This is thy people's destined way.

---

115.   **Pessach Morning.**

      Pessach Morning!
Behold God breaks our fetters;
Freedom's air we're breathing.
      Freedom's Morning!
No more affliction, no more anguish!
Wonders level Freedom's path.
      Vernal Morning!
A promised Eden radiant lies before us,
Father, Father, lead us onward!

---

116.   **The Spirit of the Age.**

To God, to God arise, my song,
  Who never gave us to despondence;
For him my flesh and spirit long.
  Who metes his mercies' great abundance?

He broke the iron rod in twain,
  Grim tyranny was swaying o'er us;
He tore asunder Egypt's chain,
  Made freedom's pillar march before us.—

O Lord, thy judgment since has tried
  Our sires with many visitations;
Nor shook their faith, e'en when they died;
  They died and blessed thy dispensations.

But on the brink of the abyss
  The trumpet of thy help was sounded;
At last we've found this home of bliss,
  By loving brothers we're surrounded.

And now, when breathing free again,
  When hate is silenced, mute the scorning,
Our spirit breaks her yoke in twain,
  And spreads her pinion toward the morning.

O grant us, Lord, to understand
  Thy deeds in their full depth and essence,
That we, uplifting heart and hand,
  In truth adore thy holy presence.

117. Praise our God.

All abroad praise our God; praise him all creation!
In all tongues, sing him songs, him alone ovation.
Bow in fear, far and near, praise him every nation!

At all times, to all climes, sendeth he good tiding.
Heart depressed findeth rest, when in him confiding,
Ne'er despair; when in care, be in God abiding.

God is nigh; hears thy cry, when storms hover o'er thee.
In distress he will bless, and send light before thee.
Hush thy grief! sure relief will to bliss restore thee.

Bend thine ear, Lord, and hear; let thy mercy heed us!
Bid thy light and thy right, on thy path to lead us!
All our days may the rays of thy wisdom speed us!

Songs for Divine Services

118.   **God, my Strength.**

O Father of all nations,
　To thee my praise shall ring,
Thine are my heart's vibrations,
　In pious lays they swing.
With joy my breast is swelling,
　Thy wonders claim my tongue.
O Lord, in mercy dwelling!
　"Jah is my strength, my song."

Thus sang our sires, delivered
　From tyranny, that day;
When they in anguish quivered,
　Wast thou their strength, their stay.
They saw thy power, thy wonder,
　And strengthened was their faith;
Thou rent'st the waves asunder,
　Mad'st in the sea a path.

Again we stand before thee,
　Redeemed from hatred's rage;
We stand here and adore thee,
　Our Rock from age to age.—
Come, let us praise his power,
　To him our thanks belong,
He is his fearers' tower,
　"Jah is their strength, their song."

(Shabuoth.)

119.   **Mount of God.**

Sinai! thou mount of God,
Sending thy rays abroad,
　Shin'st from afar.
Gav'st to the mind a light,
Showing the way of Right.
　Hallelujah!

God's everlasting laws
Are our salvation's cause.
　Give the Lord praise!
True is the Lord's command,
Through it we live, we stand;
　Praise him all days!

Thanks for the law of light,
Sent to illume our sight,
　Sing to the Lord!
Source thou of truth and grace!
Make us with love embrace
　Thy blessed word.

120.　　　　　**This Day.**

This day records the wonder,
　Lord, of the great event,
When, at thy word, asunder
　The veil of error rent.

Before thy throne of glory
　Night's phantoms took their flight,
When Israel's young and hoary
　Appeared in Horeb's sight.

With thunders promulgated,
　Thy fiery word went forth;
A light eradiated
　Illumining all earth.

Of all thy bounty's dowers
　This is my fairest part;
This feast of vernal flowers
　Uplifts to thee my heart.

O Father, thou hast bound me
  To thee with tender ties;
O Father, I have found thee,—
  My vows to thee arise.

My tongue, my tongue shall never
  Cease to proclaim thy fame;
I am thine own forever,
  Thou art my only aim.

---

121.   **On Sinai's Top.**

Rise ye all! give adoration
To the Law of revelation!
    *   *
       *

From Sinai's top a *Spring* progresses,
  That pours through all the world its flood;
The limpid current runs and blesses
  The banks it passes, with all good.
Who from this spring restores his heart,
Feels through his veins fresh vigor start.

A *Tree* of life on Sinai groweth,
  And spreads its branches far around;
No praise that human speech bestoweth
  Can ever all its beauties sound.
In dearth and want he is secured,
Who stores the fruit this tree matured.

O'er Sinai's head a *Sun* is shining
  That far abroad sends forth its rays,
Dispells dark sorrows, cheers the pining,
  Darts joy upon our earthly days.
Whose eye these heavenly rays illume,
His soul is saved and fears no doom.

Thou, Law, to us from Sinai given!
    Thou art the *Spring*, thou art the *Tree*;
Thou art the *Sun!* giv'st life from heaven
    To him who seeks life's truth in thee.
Of God and men is he beloved
Who from thy precepts never moved.

---

122.   **Up to the Lord.**

Up to the Lord arise, my song!
Resound, my lay, with harps well strung!
    God's day has come, the choicest of all days,
    Sing Hallelujah to his praise!

From heaven came in splendor bright
The Law that guideth us aright;
    Its tender beams shine on our ways,
    As in the dale the morning's rays.

It leads us o'er to heaven's domain
Through this our vale of gloom and pain,
    And consecrates our fleeting days,
    To things no time can e'er erase.

Up to the Lord arise, my song!
Resound, my lay, with harps well strung!
    God's day has come, the choicest of all days,
    Sing Hallelujah to his praise!

(New Year.)

123.   **Lord, our Creator.**

Hear us, Lord, our Creator!
To thee we send up our prayer.
Lord, Most Holy, accept our contrite confession!
    Blot out our transgression,
    And our sin make vanish.
    Give us peace eternal!

Songs for Divine Services. 65

124. **Years, like Rivers.**

Praise the Lord! The years, like rivers,
　Roll and run, and have no stay;
Leaves fall off, when autumn shivers;
　Flowers fade;—thy word stands aye.

Lord of light! Beyond glad praises,
　What can I afford to give?
But I know, the best thanks raises
　He who strives in light to live.

Lord of Light! I will not pinion
　Unto fading flowers my day;
Let me raise, in thy dominion,
　Flowers and fruits that ne'er decay.

---

125. **Days and Years.**

Ever running, ne'er delaying,
　Days and years maintain the strife,
Joys and woes, like troops arraying,—
　Friends and foes of human life.
One year more closed his career;
On his grave I linger here.

What's before me, see I not;—
　Night is o'er the pathway spun
Which to run will be my lot,
　In the year this day begun.
I can but entreat thy face,
Let me follow, Lord, thy trace!

Father, grant to me, thy servant,
　That my heart be pure within!
Aid me in my efforts fervent!
　Crush in me the power of sin!
Lead me ever by thy hand,
Till I come to heaven's land.

(Day of Atonement.)

126.   **Child's Repentance.**

O Lord, my heart is ailing,
  With sin it is oppressed;
My joys are turned to wailing,—
  How can I e'er be blessed?
Yet I have hope before me
  To health to rise again;
Thy mercy can restore me,
  And ease me of my pain.

I know since I am living,
  I oft have gone astray;
To earth my fond thoughts giving,
  I've made vain things my stay.
Not thee I sought in meekness;—
  Proud, blind, by sin beguiled,
I oft have proved my weakness.—
  I'm weaker than a child.

But children through repentance
  Can move their father's heart;
So wilt thou soften my sentence
  As I in penance smart.
My Father! I'm returning
  With tearful eyes to thee;
I know thou seest my yearning,
  Accept'st me graciously.

---

127.   **Lord, enthroned in Heaven.**

Lord, enthroned in heaven,
See, our hearts are riven
  With deep agony.
Sorrow, grief, and anguish
Make our powers languish,
  For we turned away from thee.

Should'st thou not forgive us,
And from sin relieve us,
 Lord, undone are we.
Oh, let not thy wrath sway,
From our sinful pathway
 Lead us back again to thee.

Ah, we sigh, encumbered
With our sins unnumbered;
 Whither shall we flee?
Like a reed we waver;
We have lost thy favor,
 For we turned away from thee.

But thou hast assured us,
That when sins allured us,
 We to thee might flee.
Lord, see our repentance;
Let thy pardoning sentence
 Lead us back again to thee.

---

128.   **Prayer for Peace.**

 Lord Most Holy!
Forgive us our transgressions!
Have compassion on us!
 God, Redeemer!
Hear our petition!
Wipe out the trace of guilt!
 God of mercy!
Protect us from offences!
 Grant us peace, Lord!

129. **The Memory of the Dead.**

FIRST PART.

What is life? Heir to perdition,
  Swiftly passing as a thought.
Ah! how vain is man's ambition,
  To the grave he taketh naught.

* * *

Yea, son of earth! Thou art a pilgrim here,
Worms and destruction at thy beauty jeer.

* * *

Woe! Woe!
Vain is life with all its schemes.
Woe! Woe!
Soon are over all fair dreams.

* * *

Tell me why this strain of melancholy?
  Why this fear of death and tomb?
  Why thy bosom chilled with fright?
Does no comfort beam from heavens holy?
  Comes not morning's rosy bloom
  After dark and dreary night?
Lo! One land receives the high and lowly
  Where bright light dispels all gloom,
  And destruction has no might.—
Let death come with sudden strides or slowly,
  We shall join, redeemed from doom,
  Those we love in God's true light.

* * *

Thus saith the Eternal Lord:
Unfailing is my mercy's word;
  Let in thy heart remain
    The solace I have given;
  Dust turns to dust again,
    The soul ascends to heaven.

Still your sighs, your lamentations,
 Up to heaven look with cheer!
Thither tend our aspirations;
 Why should death thrill us with fear?

Here we are but guests sojourning
 For our trial on this earth;
After death, there comes a morning
 In the country of our birth.

Part Second.

Lord, dwelling in the firmament!
 Who shall abide in thy bright tent?
And whom wilt thou forever bless,
 To see thy mount of holiness?

* *
*

Who walketh straight and acteth right;
Whose lips and heart in truth unite;
Who ne'er to slander lends his tongue;
Unto his neighbor does no wrong.

Who lowers not his brother's fame;
Feels, as his own, his brother's shame;
For vile men hath no flattering word,
But honors those who fear the Lord.

Who ne'er on usury lends his gold;
Though injured, to his oath will hold,
And take no bribe to doom the pure:
Who dealeth thus shall e'er endure.

* *
*

Let the wicked dread and shiver,
 Lest their latest hour may chime;
Woe to him whose heart's a quiver
 Stored with bolts of sin and crime.

Oh, the sweet and holy pleasure
   That awaits the good and wise!
Has their day here reached its measure,
   There a brighter day will rise.
      *   *
         *

No; I will not fear and tremble,
   When my latest hour shall chime;
Open stands for me a temple
   Wherein Virtue gleams sublime.
      *   *
         *

     Hallelujah!
Praise ye the Lord our heavenly Father,
   From night and grave he lifts us up;
His loving spirit waves; we gather
   Around his word, our staff, our hope.
     Hallelujah!
Our lives to thee be consecrated,
   While we remain on this earth's shore!
Thy glorious name be celebrated
   By earthly choirs for evermore.

---

130.   **The Day Declines.**

The day declines, the shadows grow,
   The twilight glow is kindled;
Thy grace, O Lord, on me bestow,
   Ere down my powers are dwindled,
And let me hear a voice within;
  "Thou art redeemed; forgiven thy sin."

The night is swiftly sinking down,
   The sunbeams are retreating;
O, could I mount up to thy throne
   With thee, O Father, meeting,
And learn there, by thy mercy graced:
  "Thy sin's forgiven, thy guilt effaced."

Songs for Divine Services.

The hours run fast, the minutes hie,
  Here for our prayers given;
O, use them for eternity,
  Strive for the peace from heaven,
That all your life ye hear the lay:
" How sweet, how sweet Atonement's Day!"

131. **The Peace of Neilah Evening.**

Oh the peace, when Neilah Even
  Pours its balm into the soul!
By what pains our hearts be riven:
  Prayers heal us, make us whole.

Yea, a calmness, joy-inspiring,
  Moves through our enraptured hearts,
When the sun-rays are retiring,
  And day's golden orb departs.

Lo, that is God's spirit holy,
  Harbinger of love and peace;
Comforting the meek and lowly,
  Making every sorrow cease.—

Let us bear God's dispensations,
  Let us wrestle till we're blest:
After dark and drear probations,
  Neilah comes and brings sweet rest.

(Succoth.)

132. **Thy Works proclaim.**

Thy works proclaim thy Name on earth, in heaven,
  And everywhere we see, O Lord, thy throne;
Thine are these days for our rejoicing given,
  To reap the fruits in still devotion sown.
Grant us to celebrate these hours so pleasant!
  In gratitude for all thy gifts of love:
To thee we wreathe our crowns, the Omnipresent,
  Thy grace uplifts our hearts to thee above.

133. Life a Pilgrimage.

A pilgrimage soon endēd
  Is this our earthly life;
Our huts are temporary,
Till death away shall carry
  Our souls above all strife.

But through the pilgrims' desert
  Leads us our Father's hand.
Our hut may have been cheerful,
Our lot may have been tearful;—
  We walk to heaven's land.

---

134. Festive Wreath, and Human Mission.

While, Lord, I praise thee for thy gifts' fruition,
This festive wreath shall teach my own life's mission.

  My heart! be like this Ethrog, growing
  On Hadar's tree,—with deeds o'erflowing.

  And as this Palm is upward tending,
  So be, my spirit!—never bending.

  The Myrtle sheds around sweet savor:
  My soul! What's noble shalt thou favor.

  And meek as by the brook the Willow,
  Remain, my mind, on fortune's billow.

With all my powers I will fulfill my mission,
As here I praise thee for thy gifts' fruition.

Songs for Divine Services. 73

135.   With Festive Wreaths.

With festive wreaths, Lord, we entreat thee,
Grant us with joyful hearts to meet thee,
   This Feast of Tabernacles.

We pray to thee, these emblems holding,
Lord, in thy mercy all-enfolding,
   List to our supplications!

O, bid thy tent of peace bedight us,
And let no clouds, no tempests fright us,
   Lord, in our habitations.

On earth we all with psalms adore thee,
O, let us bloom like palms before thee,
   When doffed our body's shackles.

(Feast of Conclusion.)

136.   Pleasures of Devotion.

In thy house to dwell, O Father,
   Oh, how comely and how sweet!
Happy they who cheerful gather
   To adore thy Mercy-seat.

Great things saw my soul abiding
   With thee in the festive days,
And my heart in thee confiding
   Drew sweet gladness from thy praise.

Let this cheerful spirit guide me,
   As I leave this holy shrine;
Unto thee I will confide me,
   And my life be solely thine.

(*Simchath Torah.*)

137. **This is the Torah.**

This is the Torah, this the word
　Our fathers did inherit;
Intact it was to us transferred
　Intact we will transfer it.

Uplift the Scroll, unfurl it wide,
　Let all the world look on it;
Show it, O Judah, show it with pride,
　And tell the price that won it.

Thou gav'st for this celestial good,
　Whatever mankind prizes;
Joy, riches, freedom, honor, blood—
　Who counts thy sacrifices?

This is the flag for which our sires
　Arrayed their hosts unshaken;
They went through thousand, thousand fires—
　Their flag was ne'er forsaken.

It is the same flag, Lord of might,
　Thou to their trust hast handed,
They left their lives in many a fight;—
　Here is the flag expanded.

The warriors sank around it trooped,
　Their numbers are uncounted,
The rest to power never stooped,
　Through baseness never mounted.

They passed where death had dug their bed,
　Destruction fed foes' quivers,
They passed, their banners overhead,
　Through glowing lava-rivers.

Wrapt in this flag, how many sealed
  Their faith on pyres expiring!
How many died, pierced on this shield,
  To heavenly homes retiring!

Around us furious fires did flit
  In battles unabated,
We saved the flag, God's holy **Writ,**
  The rest as naught we rated.

Therefore we have unfurled it wide,
  That all the world look on it;
We raise it high, show it with pride;
  The price was high that won it.

To God be thanks, the combats rest;
  Oh, may they rest forever!
But we will watch our sires' bequest,
  And leave our standard never.

(*Chanuckah.*)

38.   **Firmness in Faith.**

Let our day be glad or grievous,
  Prospects bright, or drear and dim,
Of his light naught shall bereave us,
  Naught shall sever us from Him.

Like our heroes firm and daring,
  Like the Maccabees of yore,
We will manly stand, declaring:
  "Thou art Lord forever more."

Thou, our Staff and Stay, wilt brace us
  Through vicissitudes of time,
And thy clemency will grace us
  Where thy glory reigns sublime.

139. My Salvation's Tower.

(After the Hebrew.)

I will praise, O Lord, thy grace,
    Fountain of all power!
Thou'rt in storms my sheltering place,
    My salvation's tower.
What if men assail me?
      God, my Lord,
      Breaks their sword,
He will never fail me.

Ever when I sighed in night,
    When the world did wound me,
God led me again to light,
    And his hand upbound me.
Darkness oft set round me,—
      He was nigh
      From on high,
And his mercy found me.

He saved me from Pharaoh's hand,
    When I cried in anguish;
Shattered Haman's haughty wand,
    As he saw me languish.—
When an enemy harmed me,
      Light and love
      From above
'Gainst his charges charmed me.

With my army God did side;—
    We, the few and humble,
Checked the Syrian's furious tide,
    Made the mighty stumble.
Heroes, young and hoary,
      Spilt their blood
      For their God,
Giving him the glory.

Cherishing a holy flame
  In their hearts unbending,
The Asmonean tribe won fame
  And renown unending.
Round their heads victorious
    Waving palms,
    Singing psalms,
Praised they God the glorious.

By the sheen of cheerful lights,
  Priests, approved in sufferings,
Came to Zion, new from fights,
  Bringing God their offerings.—
Father of Creation!
    As this night,
    Let joys light,
Ever crown thy nation!

VI.

THE SEASONS OF THE YEAR.

140. **The Beneficence of the Lord.**

The heavens and the earth, O Lord,
   Are full of thy beneficence;
The worlds, so vast and wondrous, say,
   "We are His handiwork."

---

141. **Spring.**

Up, praise Him for the beauteous Spring
   And all its bloomy treasures!—
Whose love bids all creation sing
   And fills each heart with pleasures.

Shout to the Lord a joyous lay,
   Whose bounteous voice reviveth
What seemed forever to decay,
   That in new bloom it thriveth.

From all these beauties here on earth
   Lift up your eyes to heaven!
In sweet accord with Nature's mirth,
   To God be praises given!

142. Summer.

To the Father of all creatures
    Soar, my thoughts, to seek his face!
Lawn and field wear joyous features,
    Telling his unbounded grace.

Nature round me sprouting, blooming,
    Speaks aloud of life's sweet zest;
Kindles flames of joy, consuming
    Every grief within my breast.

Lord! I praise thy all-renewing,
    Life-bestowing power and love;
Thanks and joys, all cares subduing,
    Lift my heart to thee above.

143. Autumn.

Lo, Autumn's pale, yet charming light
    Lends to the field new graces;
In dying Nature, Lord of Might,
    We still see thy love's traces.

Autumn is like a pious life,
    That blesses till it closes;
When ended is life's toil and strife,
    Of bliss it still disposes.

144. Winter.

Be blessèd, Lord, Rock of all ages,
    Whose loving-kindness hath no term.
What if the storm of winter rages?
    It is to wake the slumbering germ.
        Comes the Spring, the all-reviving,
        Earth shows forth her secret thriving.

Thy mercies, Lord, endure for ever.—
When Winter sends his freezing breath,
And in the bed that warmeth never,
We rest, wrapt in the shroud of death:
Lord, thy breath goes forth, reviving
Death-bound souls for vernal thriving.

145. **Nature, God's Witness.**

Who spake, and the earth was moulded,
And the heavens were unfolded?
And who commands the legions
Of lights in unsearched regions?

My body—who did make it,
And who to life awake it?
Who taught my soul immortal
To enter wisdom's portal?

'Tis thou! thy works proclaim thee,
"The Bountiful" they name thee.
My spirit hears their voices,
And in their praise rejoices.

VII.

SONGS FOR THE CONFIRMATION ACT.

146.   **Moment most holy.**

Confirmands.

Blessèd, O blessèd,
  Moment most holy,
Leading the lowly
  Youth to the Lord!

Choir.

Pray for his light!
  Nigh is he e'er
To the contrite;
  Children in prayer
Are his delight.

Confirmands.

Bounteous Father!
  In thy light lead us,
From thy height heed us!
  Thou art our Shepherd,
We are thy flock.

Choir.

Be not in fright!
  Nigh is he e'er
To the contrite;
  Children in prayer
Are his delight.

Confirmands.

Make us victorious,
    While here we strive,
Till at thy glorious
    Throne we arrive.

---

147.   **Be blessed, O Lord.**

Choir.

Be blessèd, O Lord,
Whose loving-kindness
Gave laws of wisdom,
To lead our children
In salvation's path.

Reader's Solo.

Be blessèd, O Lord!
This solemn moment
Will lead our children
To life eternal
Through thy covenant.

Confirmands.

We bless thee, O Lord!
The vows we offer
Here in thy dwelling,
Shall in our bosoms
Live forever more.   Amen.

Songs for Divine Services.

148.   **Our Lips shall praise Thee.**

Our lips shall praise thee, Lord of Mercy!
  Who know'st each heart, its joys and cares,
Who guidest by thy light the pilgrim,
  When dark his path and full of snares.

Our lips shall praise thee, Holy Being!
  Whose ways are just, and yet so mild!
We are thy children; thou did'st choose us,
  Who ne'er forsak'st a praying child.

With all our hearts we love thee, Father!
  With all our souls we will be thine;
In smiling sunshine we will love thee;
  We'll love thee, should our sun decline.

We will forever be thy servants,
  And cheerfully obey thy will;
Thy law, thy light shall ever guide us:
  What thou command'st, we will fulfill.

---

149.   **The Teachings of the Lord.**

Happy ye who learn the teachings
  Of the Lord, in guileless youth!
Lofty are the young soul's reachings,
  And her aim is living truth.

Happy fields that in good season
  Have received a holy seed!
Happy ye whose youthful reason
  Has conceived a holy creed.

These thy children,—Father, heed them,
  Be their trust and staff of life;
On the path of virtue lead them,
  Through this world with dangers rife.

150. We pray.

We pray thee, Father, hide us
    Beneath thy MERCY's shade,
And in thy pathway guide us;
    Withhold not, Lord, thine aid.

We pray thee, Father, brighten
    With TRUTH our errors' night;
Thou only canst enlighten;
    "In thy light we see light."

We pray thee, Father, quiet
    Our hearts with heavenly PEACE.
And bid the stormy riot
    Of earthly lusts to cease.

We pray thee, Lord, assist us
    With STRENGTH, for we are weak;
Whene'er good deeds enlist us,
    O come and help the meek.

We pray thee, let thy BLESSING
    Descend on us this day,
That we, thy grace possessing,
    May follow thee for aye.

151.   Grateful Praises.

O holy joy that raises
  Again each praying heart!
Give to the Lord new praises,
  Ere from this house ye part.
Good seeds have been implanted
  In bosoms young and pure;
Let growth to them be granted,
  O Lord, make them mature!

O, what a heavenly blessing
  Moves over us this hour!
O joy! we are possessing
  A new and holier power.
O Father, make us willing
  To glorify thy name
Through deeds of truth, fulfilling
  The Law thou didst proclaim.

Like shadows days are flying,
  Thou, Lord, wilt e'er endure;
A fountain never drying
  Is thy word, clear and pure.
To thee, the bounteous donor
  Of truths that never end,
Shall songs of praise and honor
  From pious lips ascend.

152. Come, ye Children.

Choir.

Come, ye children, to his house,
    Come with holy joy before him.—
Here profess your pious vows;
    God will hear you; come, implore him.

Confirmands.

With joy we come before his throne,
    And with our vows draw near him,
To be his servants, his alone,
    Who loveth all that fear him.

He knows what longing in us dwells,
    He knows what we endeavor,
Knows our desire, above all else
    In truth to live forever.

Unto the Lord we consecrate
    Ourselves and all within us,
O may his light irradiate
    Our souls, for truth to win us.

Choir.

Raising up to thee their voices,
    Here this day thy children stand;
With thy light, Lord, that rejoices
    Pious souls, O bless this band.

Confirmands.

Raising up to thee our voices,
    We, thy suppliants, now ask,
Father, with thy light rejoice us,
    In whose rays thy fearers bask.

What we in our bosoms cherish,
  Lord, before thee now we own;
Truths and hopes that never perish,
  We lay down before thy throne.

We will, guided by thy spirit,
  Live and die, O Lord, with thee;
Father, cause us to inherit
  Thy true grace eternally.

Choir.

Ye have brought your holy vows
Here before him, in his house;—
  Go, and be blest fore'er!
  Yours be a happy share,
  Yours be a pleasant lot:
    May peace from heaven,
  And faith that shaketh not,
    To you be given!

VIII.
FOR THE THANKSGIVING DAY.

153. **The Thanks of all Living.**

Almighty Lord, who sendest forth thy breath,
   Into existence waking lives unnumbered;
With all that gives them happiness beneath
   They are by thy paternal care remembered.
In filial love therefore, thy Name is blest
By all that breathe, enjoying life's sweet zest.

And all look up with never failing trust
   To thy paternal grace, the all-sustaining.
Lord! Who that lives should not bow down in dust
   To thee whose faith and love are never waning?
Lo, gratitude is to thy name addressed
By all that breathe, enjoying life's sweet zest.

O Father, let the lustre of thy face
   Beam to all souls that for thee wait confiding,
And let all hearts that sing thy loving-grace
   Behold thy mercy in their midst abiding.
O Lord, let thy compassion ever rest
On all that breathe, enjoying life's sweet zest!

154. The Mercies of the Lord.

Days and nights upon us shower,
    Lord, the mercies of thy choice;
What restores the body's power,
    And what makes the soul rejoice,
Is in thy creation stored.
Everywhere, I find, O Lord,
Of thy love divine a token,
Giving me delights unspoken.

Through thy grace the trees have yielded
    Fruits, the panting to sustain,
And the flowing fields were gilded
    With the ears of ripened grain.
Blest with plenty, Earth can give
Food to all that on her live.
Seeing, Lord, thy love abundant,
Who could ever be despondent?

All our anthems of devotion,
    How they are inadequate
To express our heart's emotion,
    Lord, for whom all creatures wait!
Thou'rt our guardian, thou our guide,
Thou wilt e'er with us abide;
E'en in trials and distresses
Thy paternal mercies bless us.

155.   Our Country.

Protect us, Father, be our stay!
O keep us safe from day to day.
   Let order reign in our dear land,
   And bless the labor of each hand.

The mighty States together bound,
O, let them rest on firmest ground:
   On truth and justice let them rest,
   With freedom and with concord blest.

Our leaders, Lord, do thou inspire
With zeal and strength that never tire;
   Around our nation wreathe the band
   Of common love to our dear land.

Bid freedom and the reign of peace
Among all human kind increase.
   Thy praise be told by every mouth,
   From East to West, from North to South!

PRAYERS AND MEDITATIONS.

ON THE EVE OF THE NEW YEAR.

The Rabbi.

Out of the depths of our hearts do we call on thee, O Lord! O God, hear our prayer and accept our supplication!

We have come this night before thy throne to render praise and adoration unto thy Name. We bring unto thee the thankful offerings of our lips for the numberless gifts of thy bounty, and beseech thee to grant us, in the coming year, life and prosperity, blessing and contentment.

And we have all come with trust in thy mercy, and wait for thy grace. We all lift up our eyes unto thee, as children wait for their father's loving gaze. When we look backward on the past year and the many joys and pains it brought unto us, and when we look forward into the dark vista of the new year, considering what joys and pains it may contain for us, we perceive and acknowledge that our destinies are in thy hand, and that mercy and kindness are with thee. Therefore do we put our trust in thee.; therefore do we pour out our souls before thee, when, on the entrance of a new period of existence, our emotions overwhelm us.

Be pleased, then, to accept the thanks which we render unto thee for so many a joy, so many a relief, so many a blessing bestowed on us during the year just faded from sight.

Accept also the thanks which, with a submissive heart, we render unto thee even for the trials with which thou didst visit us, for the woes wherewith thou didst see fit to afflict us, the sorrowful burdens thou didst place upon us, in order that we might be cleansed and purified from all that is sinful and debasing, and be led in meekness unto thee, the Master of all beings.

Accept also the thanks which we lay upon thy altar for the undertakings on behalf of the general welfare wherein we have been allowed to share, aiding in a union for common interests which thou hast permitted us to attain,—partaking in so many movements for the advancement of Israel's cause which thy voice aroused in our hearts.

O, do thou further look with grace upon us in this year just ushered in; let the abundance of thy blessings rest upon us, so that it may become a year of life and health to all that call on thee,—a year of peace and concord to all that acknowledge thee,—a year in which the true divine spirit is aroused in the midst of Israel,—a year of increased love and fear of thy Holy Name, and of esteem and appreciation of us, the standard bearers of thy unity over the whole face of the earth.

Happy as we, in this our country, are in the enjoyment of liberty, shared in common by all, we call to mind this night our brethren in faith who are yet refused those inherent rights because of their religious convictions. O, grant that everywhere on earth Israel's sons may be relieved of the heavy and painful burden of oppression which has its origin in the olden days of prejudice; grant that in every spot, as here, the barriers may be torn down which separate the professors of thy unity from those whom we are taught to call our brethren, and by whom we desire to be called brethren in union and friendship. O, grant that the knowledge of thy Name and the consciousness of equality as the inalienable right of every human being, may be kindled, and shine resplendently among all nations.

O, destroy the seeds of discord between man and man, between people and people, out of which grow the thorns of strife and the thistles of war. Let the seeds of love and humanity which thou hast strewed, both in thy divine word and in the uncorrupted heart of man, spring up and flourish, in order that all beings whom thou hast endowed with reason, may extend a brotherly hand to each other, and unite in thy Name and in thy fear, as thou hast promised through thy prophets.

And, thus, be thou praised, O Lord Eternal, who in grace and mercy hearest the prayers of all who call on thee in truth! Amen.

Choir.

Hear us, as in thy dwelling
   We grateful sing thy love,
Our songs of praise rise swelling
   Unto thy throne above.
Our knees before thee bended,
   We pray in holy fear:
Let all our woes be ended
   With the expiring year.

Bring near the day, O Father,
   When every lip names thee,
In love all nations gather
   And bid all contests flee.
Let Israel's sons a blessing
   To all mankind appear,
Show all that they're possessing
   Thy grace this coming year.

BEFORE SOUNDING THE SHOFAR.

The Rabbi.

"Awake, ye slumberers, from your slumbers, and ye listless ones from your indifference; examine your deeds, and penitently return to the Source of justice and truth. O ye, that, immerged in worldly employments and pleasures, forget your true destiny; ye who pass your days in vanities which cannot profit nor deliver—O, remember your Creator; look into your own souls, and amend your ways and your deeds. Let each of you abandon his bad course and ignoble thoughts!"

This is the Shofar's admonition, as interpreted by one of our Sages.

O Lord our God! Should we hear the call and not tremble?—The piercing sound of the cornet reverberating on our ear, we are made conscious that we have oft forgotten the high mission of humanity for which thou hast placed us on earth; that we have oft been heedless of the lofty career which thy law has pointed out before us; that we have oft disregarded thy divine voice within us cautioning our souls against self-degradation and wrong-doing, and inciting us to self-elevation and noble deeds.

The Shofar's sound is unto us a symbol of thy forcible appeal unto the children of men. We hear thy voice, O Father; thou callest thy children back to thee, and we will readily obey thy summons.

We venture this day to approach thee with the Shofar's thrilling sound ascending as the homage we bring unto thee. Thou art our King, and we are thy servants; thou our Master, and we the messengers of thy will; thou our Father, and we thy children. O, grant that our whole earthly existence may be one continuous glorification unto thee and homage rendered unto thy great Name, and that all our steps may manifest that they are regulated by thy commands alone.

Thou art the Judge of our actions, and our deeds lie open before thee as a book of records; thou art the director of our destinies and dispensest to each according to thy wisdom, justice and kindness. O, judge us not according to our doings; let thy grace reign over us; forgive our failings, and pardon our sins! When thou goest with us into judgment, O let us appear before thee cleansed and purified from all defilement; for thou art the God of love, and with thee there is redemption.

Grant, then, that the tones of the Shofar may enter into our hearts and awaken therein all the noble resolves and sublime vows to which thy voice summons us; and like our fathers before the height of Sinai, when they were aroused by the sound of the Shofar, so will we exclaim, "Whatever the admonition of the Lord requires of us, we will do in humble obedience." Amen.

⸻

The trumpet calls, "Awake, awake,
    List to my warning voice;
Inspect thy ways; the bad forsake,
    And make the good thy choice."

We hear thy voice; O Lord, we're called
    Before thy court divine;
We hear thy voice and stand appalled,
    And in our sins we pine.

Judge us according to thy grace,
    Not as our deeds deserve;
Make us endure before thy face,
    And ne'er more from thee swerve.

FOR THE MEMORIAL SERVICE FOR THE DEAD.

Rabbi.

A sad, and yet a blissful hour is it, when on the holiest of days—on the Sabbath of Sabbaths—our souls soar upward to the realms above where perpetual Sabbath reigns,—where the toil of life is over, and man enjoys the fruits of his work on earth.

The seal of mystery is stamped on the futurity of man's soul. None living has ever penetrated it, and of the departed none has returned to give knowledge of what he has seen, and to answer the solemn questions that fill every human being with anxiety. No prophet in holy vision has rent the veil asunder which is drawn over the life of mortals. " No eye has ever seen, besides God alone, what is prepared for those that wait for him."

But an inner voice, loud and intelligible, tells us that this life here, full as it is of toil and trouble, of contention and strife, of trial and temptation, cannot be closed with the death of the body. It *cannot* be that we should be delivered up to destruction as soon as the body is placed in the silent grave. It *cannot* be that we should here strive and wrestle in vain, while naught remains of us but the vanities for which we have so strenuously toiled. It *cannot* be that both good and bad—the noble and the mean,—he that all his life-time has striven for virtue, and he that has been a slave of brutal passions,—he that in noble self-denial has loved mankind and devoted his best powers to their welfare, and he that in vile selfishness has looked upon the world as his dominion to be despoiled by him in injustice and violence,—it *cannot* be that all should be alike subject to destruction and annihilation.

A sure conviction fills our hearts that those who in tears have here strewn seeds of virtue, will in future reap the fruit of gladness; who here contended with sin and conquered, will one day enjoy the results of their victory; who here through struggle and trials have purified and cleansed themselves, will rejoice in the realization of beatitude. Such conviction speaks to man's soul: "Fear not! there is a reward for thy work; there is a hope for thy future which cannot fail!"

And this conviction of immortality which the Creator of the universe has placed in our minds,—this surety which thrills our bosoms, is the surest evidence of the immortality of the soul.

What understanding builds up, understanding may tear down again; what reason developes, reason may refute; but the presentiment which reaches conviction, cannot be implanted in our breast for our deception. The longing which the All-bountiful has placed in our hearts, *must* be fulfilled. This struggle, this striving on earth, *must* find a reward,—a reward, not of an earthly nature, as the struggle and strife are not of this earth. This flame that turneth upwards, must eventually reach the great Source of light.

Yea, Eternal Lord, this day which, in its blissful sanctity, is itself a messenger from heaven, calling our souls away from what is perishable, and directing them towards what is eternal,—this day is pre-eminently adapted to confirm within us the conviction that thou hast breathed an immortal spirit into our bodies, and that it is thou who recallest it when its earthly mission is fulfilled. This day of expiation whereon the triumph of the soul over the body is celebrated, seems unto us like a mirror reflecting its very life, when no longer chained by corporeal bonds. This day is unto us a greeting from yonder realms to which our holy presentiment is pointing.

And ye, O dear departed ones, united with whom

we here on earth once walked, until the voice of the Lord summoned you away! Ye, our beloved, whose affection made us happy, whose watchful care protected us, whose instruction fitted us for our career, whose example shone before us; ye who quickened us with your word, encouraged us with your comfort; all ye whose existence beautified ours, and ye whose anticipated future shed a halo over our path,—and whose departure gave us unutterable grief! ye, never forgotten objects of our affection and our longing!—ye stand this moment before our mental gaze. Death has not rent asunder the ties which life had woven; the gloomy grave cannot obscure the light that illuminated your existence. *Your* souls are descending unto us; *our* souls are soaring up to you. Our remembrance of you, mingled with sweetness and sadness, is our staff and stay on our earthly pilgrimage, our shield and buckler amid our battles,—our strength and animation in all our strivings. Our grief at your departure from us, cleanses and purifies our souls; our affliction is a sweet angel bringing peace and reconciliation into our homes; our longing uplifteth us above the vanities of this earth, turning our hearts toward the things imperishable.

And in this refined and blissful state of our souls, are we enabled, on this day of confession and repentance, to rise from the humiliating consciousness of sin unto the firm resolve that we will devote our lives to the service of God and humanity in truth and uprightness; that we will renew the combat against sin and temptation; that we will cleanse our hearts from the dross of selfishness; and that we will render ourselves worthy to appear before the Supreme Judge on the day he summons us unto life eternal. Amen.

(The remainder of the Memorial Service see Prayer Book, p. 384 and following.)

PRAYERS FOR VARIOUS OCCASIONS.

Prayer of a Husband for Sustenance and Domestic Happiness.

O Lord and Father, who givest food unto all creatures, and in thy abundant love providest for myriads of beings! grant that I and my family may likewise find the needful support of life. I pray not for extensive riches or possessions, but give me, O Father, what I really need, and what is good and beneficial for me. Guard me, All-bountiful God, from want and privation, and direct thou my heart, that in my pursuit after the requirements of this life, I may never deviate from the path of righteousness. Endow me with a contented heart, that I may in tranquillity and happiness enjoy the fruition of thy merciful gifts.

Vouchsafe, O Lord, unto me the means of aiding my poor and needy fellow-beings, according to the best impulses of my heart, and let my habitation ever be open to the distressed and afflicted, that they may find there comfort and relief.

Be further pleased, O Father, to grant unto all my dear ones the great blessing of health; keep aloof from us sickness and woe. Grant that true piety may ever reign in my household and in the hearts of my kindred. (And especially do I beseech thee to vouchsafe, that my beloved children whom thou hast been pleased to entrust to my care and guardianship, may grow up as good men and women, and true Israelites. Give them success and prosperity in their undertakings, and guard them from the manifold dangers ever impending over man's life, that they may never go astray, but ever through deeds of virtue and truth glorify thy Name, deserve honor for themselves, and crown my life with unpurchasable joy.) Amen.

Prayer of a Wife.

Father of Mercy! Unto thee my heart is turned; unto thy loving care I resign what is dearest to me on earth. Protect my dear husband (and children), every member of my household, and all my family. Let thy loving watchfulness rest over them and defend them from whatever evil may threaten them by night or by day. Keep far from us disease and suffering, that we may not live in fear of the dangers of the day or the terrors of the night. Command thy angels to guard us in all our ways. Assist me in watching over the inclinations of my heart and my conduct in life. Guard me from vanity and worldliness; teach me, in true womanhood,—in chastity and simplicity, to seek and find my highest gratifications in the innocent enjoyments of home. Grant unto me and my kindred, health of body, and keep our souls aloof from sinful allurements and temptations. Let us find favor, both in thy sight, and in the eyes of the good among mankind. Preserve my husband unto me in life and health; for what would I, the feeble woman, be, if bereft of his support? Keep watch over our domestic happiness and peace, and grant unto us all eternal salvation. Accept this my prayer unto thee, who art my Stay and my Hope forever. Amen.

Prayer of a Mother when Visiting the House of God after her Confinement.

O Lord, thou art exalted above all, and yet nigh unto those who, in truth and devotion, call on thee! With a humble and joyful heart, do I appear before thee to lay on thy altar my offering of thanks for thy aid and assistance, thy help and protection, who wert with me in my hour of need, didst guard me when death seemed to impend, and human strength to fail. O Lord, from a true heart do I thank thee for the addition to my domestic happiness.

O may the sweet hopes which now thrill my bosom never be disappointed! Watch over my tender babe, that it may thrive both in mind and body. Give me strength that I may be able at all times to perform my maternal duties, without neglecting any of them for the desire of enjoyment or by reason of bodily weakness. Give me wisdom to fulfill the responsible task of training the child thou hast given me, and aid me with thy wisdom and mercy, should either my power fail or inclination waver. Accept my solemn vow, that I will instruct my child in thy Law, that it may be armed with that knowledge which surpasses all other, so as to be able in due time to resist allurement, and become rich in virtue, and reverence of thee. Bountiful Father, bless and preserve it, that it may grow up in happiness, realizing our hopes, and glorifying thy Name. Amen.

Prayer for a Sick Person.

Almighty God! Hear the prayer which I offer unto thee on behalf of a suffering friend. Have compassion on him (her), and send him (her) thine aid. Let his (her) affliction come before thee, and his (her) prayer ascend unto thy throne. His (her) eyes being lifted up to thee, O turn unto him (her), in thy mercy, for thou art the healer of the sick and a faithful attendant of the suffering.

Should it however be thy inscrutable will that suffering should continue to be his (her) portion, O, do thou inspire him (her) with resignation to thy decrees, trust in thy dispensations, and never-ceasing hope in thee and thy goodness. But, O let his (her) life be spared, merciful Lord! Vouchsafe unto the wearied limbs new strength, re-animate his (her) depressed heart, and grant that my dear friend may again enter on the path of renewed life in joy and happiness. Amen.

FOR THE CONFIRMATION RITES.

Prayer of the Confirmands.

All-bountiful Father! With filial reverence do we approach thee at this solemn hour to consecrate our hearts unto thy service. Thou hast been with us, since we first beheld the light of day; thou hast preserved us from evil and from sickness, and up to this moment thy loving hand has led us, as a father leadeth his child. We thank thee, O Lord, for thy goodness, which we will never forget throughout all our days.

Thou hast given us dear parents, guardians and leaders, who have confirmed us in all that is good, showing us the path that leads unto thee. How can we adequately thank thee for all this?—Advancing now from the period of childhood, we promise to obey thee, O God, and keep thy commandments.

But do thou still continue thy guardianship, and strengthen us to live in thy sight as virtuous children and pious Israelites.

Be specially with us in this hour, O Omnipresent Being! Strengthen our hearts, that we may perceive and understand the significance of this moment unto all future days. Remove now from our minds all extraneous and wanton thoughts, and let our full attention be turned to the sacredness of this period. Preserve within us forever the earnest emotions now alive in our hearts, that from this hour we may date a healthful change in our conduct; that we may wax more thoughtful, virtuous, and obedient to thee, our Lord and Father! Amen.

Prayer of a single Confirmand.

Bountiful Father! With deep gratitude do I acknowledge thy infinite mercy, Thou hast enlightened me in thy Law, which teaches me what to perform and what to avoid. I know now whereon my happiness depends; give me, therefore, strength to strive for it without deviating to the right or to the left.

Soon am I to enter into active life, where there are dangers and temptations constantly lurking. O Lord, aid me, that I may tread firmly on the head of sin, ere he wound my foot and gain the mastery over me.

As I'am now realizing what gratitude I owe to thee, O Lord, and to my dear parents (guardians), O grant that the memory of these benefits may never cease to animate me with strength, in order that I may remain virtuous in the hour of temptation. Then shall I never sin, never act against thy will, nor grieve my dear ones through ungodly conduct or through moral weakness and deviation from the path of rectitude.

Reviewing the past period of my life, I am filled with trust for my future, for we are assured, O Lord, that thou art ever nigh unto all that seek thee in truth. I do seek thee, O Father; O let me then find thee! Enlighten me with thy holy spirit, strengthen me with thy divine aid, and let me always live full of trust and belief in thee, O Father! Amen.

Confession of Faith.

We firmly and truly believe that God is One, the only Lord,--a pure, spiritual Being; that God is the Creator, Ruler and Sustainer of the universe. To him alone, and none besides, is it proper to give praise and adoration, thanks and glory.

We firmly and truly believe that God has created man in his own image, endowing him with reason and free will, and placing in his heart the desire for perfection.

We firmly and truly believe that God has revealed to man discrimination between right and wrong, by implanting within him the consciousness of his mission for morality, and causing the voice of conscience to speak within him in accents of caution and admonition—furthermore, that on Israel has he specially bestowed the light of divine revelation, when he redeemed them from Egyptian thralldom, and imparted to them the Law of truth, through his servant Moses, on Mount Sinai.

We firmly and truly believe that the soul that God has breathed into us, is *immortal* and destined for future life, when it shall be judged for its doings, to be rewarded with imperishable happiness for the good it may have achieved on earth, and punished, according to the wisdom and justice of the Lord, for the evil it may have committed.

We firmly and truly believe that God has chosen Israel to be a nation of priests among all mankind,— that Israel, by means of the revelation on Sinai, have received the sublime mission of spreading over all the earth the truths there made known, and of confirming all mankind in the true knowledge of God,—thus establishing his divine kingdom on earth.

We firmly and truly believe that the *Messianic Days* predicted by our prophets, will finally be realized through Israel's mission, when all mankind, redeemed from error, shall acknowledge the Only God as their Creator, Father and Redeemer. On that day shall all in unity and concord exclaim, "The Lord is One, and his Name One."

Deeply imbued with the truth of these principles, we solemnly vow ever to confess them before all men in sincerity and frankness. We will live and die as Israelites, and with our latest breath seal the cardinal truth of our holy faith:

שְׁמַע יִשְׂרָאֵל. יְיָ אֱלֹהֵינוּ. יְיָ אֶחָד:

HEAR, O ISRAEL, THE LORD OUR GOD, THE LORD IS ONE.